THE JAMES BOND LOVER'S GUIDE TO BRITAIN

THE JAMES BOND LOVER'S GUIDE TO BRITAIN

EDWARD BIDDULPH

WHITE OWL
AN IMPRINT OF PEN & SWORD BOOKS LTD.
YORKSHIRE – PHILADELPHIA

First published in Great Britain in 2025 by
White Owl
An imprint of
Pen & Sword Books Ltd.
Yorkshire - Philadelphia

ISBN 978 1 03611 645 3

A CIP catalogue record for this book is available from the British Library.

Design: SJmagic DESIGN SERVICES, India.

The Publisher's authorised representative in the EU for product safety is Authorised Rep Compliance Ltd., Ground Floor, 71 Lower Baggot Street, Dublin D02 P593, Ireland.
www.arccompliance.com

For a complete list of Pen & Sword titles please contact

PEN & SWORD BOOKS LIMITED
George House, Beevor Street, Off Pontefract Road, Hoyle Mill, Barnsley, South Yorkshire, England, S71 1HN.
E-mail: enquiries@pen-and-sword.co.uk
Website: www.pen-and-sword.co.uk

or

PEN AND SWORD BOOKS
1950 Lawrence Rd, Havertown, PA 19083, USA
E-mail: uspen-and-sword@casematepublishers.com
Website: www.penandswordbooks.com

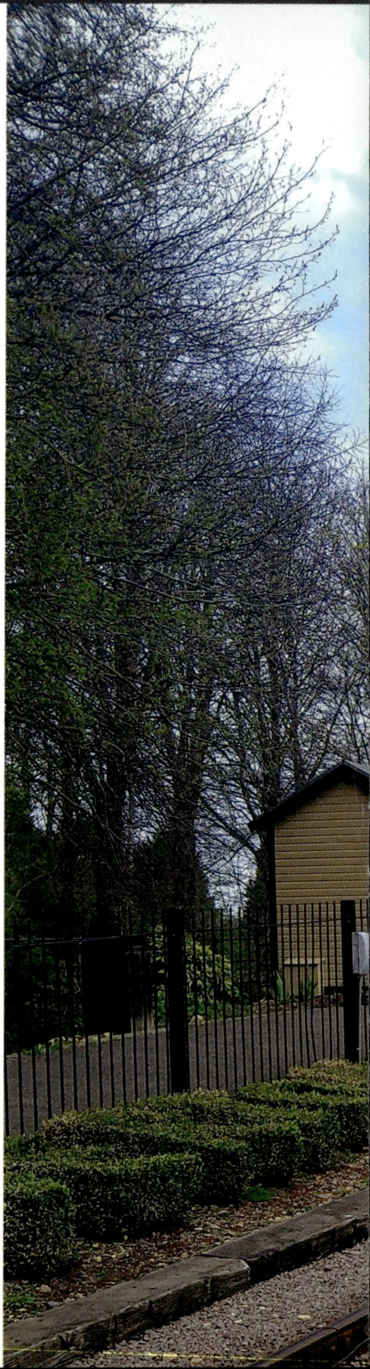

CONTENTS

ACKNOWLEDGEMENTS

I am enormously grateful to David Leigh (www.thejamesbonddossier.com) and David Lowbridge-Ellis MBE (www.licencetoqueer.com) for their comments and corrections on drafts of this book. Any errors that remain are, of course, the responsibility of the author alone. I would also like to thank Charles Rousseaux for preparing the maps, Joyce Compton for providing information on, and a photograph of, Blaen-y-pant House, and Rob Glew for the photograph of Liverpool Road, Chester. My thanks also go to Chelsea historian Ian Foster for information on Cheyne Walk, and I owe a debt of gratitude to the Past Preservers Casting team and staff at Pen & Sword Books, particularly Charlotte Mitchell, Janet Brookes and Olivia Camozzi-Jones. This book would not have been completed without the support of my wife Kim and daughter Katharine, who not only encouraged my writing, but also accompanied me on my tour of Bond's Britain to research the various sites. I owe them a debt of gratitude and it is to them that the book is dedicated. All images were taken by me, unless otherwise indicated.

INTRODUCTION

Where might we situate the essential landscape – the Bondscape, if you prefer – of James Bond? The snow-covered mountains of Switzerland and Austria? The hot and steamy coastlines of the Caribbean? The sophisticated pleasure-spots of Montenegro and Monaco? The cold, silent majesty of space? All the above, certainly, but what about Britain? Britain probably would not be the first place that one would associate with Bond, despite his being as quintessential a British character as Sherlock Holmes. He is, after all, an MI6 officer and would not expect to operate on home turf. Yet Britain, whether providing principal locations, as in the novel of *Moonraker* or the film of SKYFALL, or doubling surprisingly convincingly for much more exotic climes, forms the backdrop of practically every Bond adventure.

If the map of locations connected to the James Bond books and films does not quite stretch from John O'Groats to Land's End, it comes very close. *The James Bond Lover's Guide to Britain* describes more than 150 Bond-related sites and places, from the Western Highlands of Scotland to St Ives in the south-western tip of Cornwall. It is not the first book to explore the physical landscape of the world's most famous fictional spy, but it is perhaps alone in its aim of showcasing in a single volume not only locations in Britain associated with the film series – chiefly the films made by EON Productions – but also the series of novels by James Bond creator Ian Fleming. In addition, the book highlights sites that are off the well-beaten Bondian track, places that inspired Ian Fleming's writing, such as Enton Hall, near Godalming in Surrey, which was the basis for the Shrublands health clinic in *Thunderball*, or otherwise have something to interest the James Bond lover, such as the Royal Armouries Museum in Leeds, which brings together in one of its displays weapons that feature in the books and films. The result is a guidebook that demonstrates that in Britain one is never far from a place with a connection to James Bond, and that James Bond is truly a national figure.

In preparing this book, I have made discoveries too. In my professional life, I am an archaeologist, analysing and bringing to publication the results of archaeological fieldwork. With the first Bond novel, *Casino Royale*, reaching its seventieth anniversary in 2023 and the first Bond film, DR NO, its sixtieth anniversary in 2022, the novels and films can themselves seem like historical resources, preserving in their descriptions or on film traces of

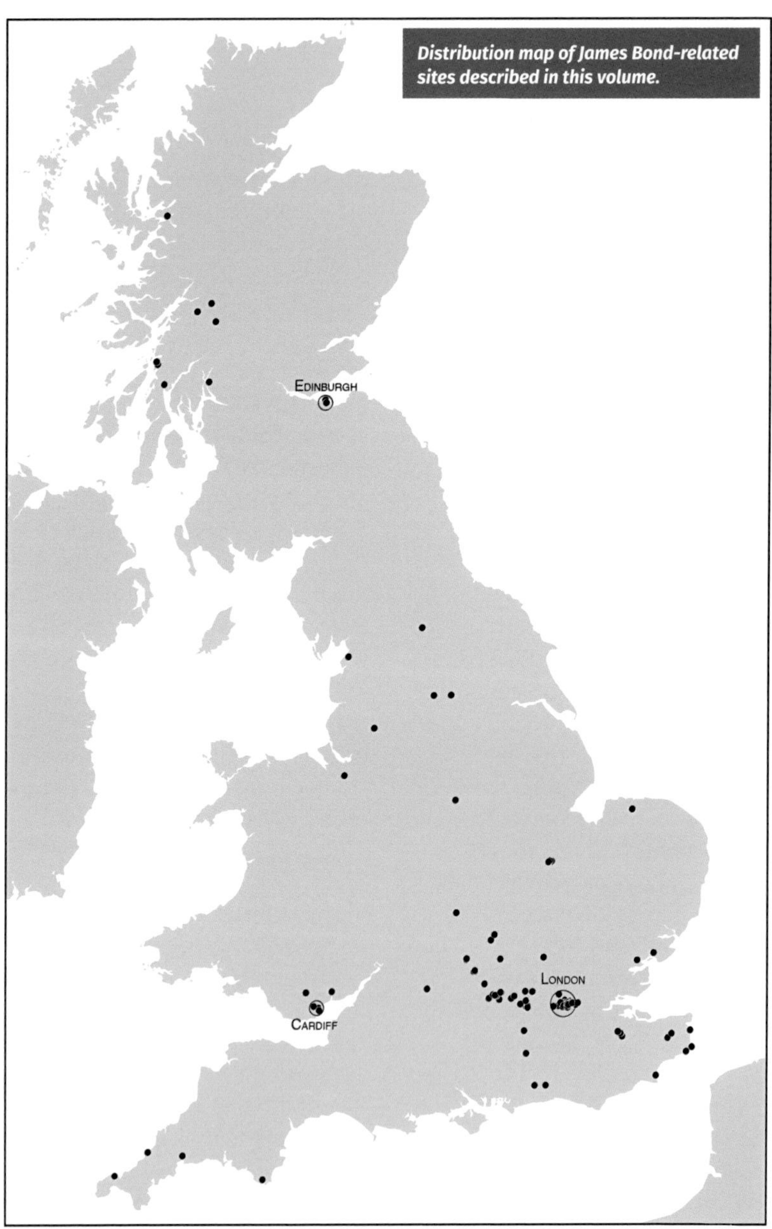

Distribution map of James Bond-related sites described in this volume.

places that have now changed beyond recognition. An obvious change, for example, has been the construction of the motorway system, which did not exist when Ian Fleming began writing. When James Bond motors from London to Deal in Kent in *Moonraker*, he takes a route that today would never be shown on any satellite navigation system except after several wrong turns, and in any case cannot be followed without diversions. I have used my archaeological skills – visiting the sites, studying old maps, digging into documentary archives – to identify changes in the landscape and point the reader to the scene as James Bond would have seen it.

This book is for anyone who is curious about the British locations that appear in the films or are mentioned in the novels. Which Scottish mountain road do James Bond and M stop at in SKYFALL? Where did James Bond splash the traffic wardens in THE WORLD IS NOT ENOUGH? Where does the James Bond of the novels live? The answers to these questions and more can be discovered within these pages. Many sites coincide with restaurants, museums, historic houses, or other visitor attractions, offering plenty of opportunities to include Bondian sightseeing in dining-out plans, holiday trips or weekend getaways. Some of the locations provide the chance for James Bond lovers to experience something of the James Bond lifestyle or recreate scenes from the films. If you want to dine like Bond, then a meal at Scott's or Rules in London is a must. If you would like to pretend you are being chased by a renegade Russian general in OCTOPUSSY, then take a ride on a vintage train on the Nene Valley Railway. Several locations are hotels or available to hire as holiday cottages, making it possible not only to visit the locations, but stay there as well.

While visiting these locations, James Bond lovers will discover that their hero has left his mark on the landscape. At Amberley Museum in West Sussex, the time that Roger Moore visited the former chalk quarry to film scenes for A VIEW TO A KILL is remembered with information panels and the display of mining wagons that appeared on screen. Ian Fleming's links with Kent are commemorated by a statue of the author on Dover beach. These remind us that the legacy of Ian Fleming's creation is not only evident in the continued popularity of the books and films, but also in our physical environment.

All novels are in italics (for example *On Her Majesty's Secret Service*), while all film titles are in capitals (thus, ON HER MAJESTY'S SECRET SERVICE). Sites are arranged by nation – sub-divided in England into standard English regions – and then by county or London borough. Within each county or borough, sites are placed into rough geographical groupings; for example, under Oxfordshire, all sites in Oxford are grouped together. A postcode is provided for each entry, although for some entries, for example those in the countryside away from buildings, the postcode is an approximate indication of the location. Sites are accessible by car, at least most of the way; some require a short walk after parking one's vehicle. If travelling by public transport, do check local services for routes and timetables. Ordnance Survey maps may be useful for rural sites, and I have provided grid references as well as postcodes for the more remote locations. Do also check before travelling that the public houses, hotels, restaurants, and so on are open to the public. Even iconic places may periodically be closed to the public, among them Stoke Park, the scene of James Bond's famous golf match in GOLDFINGER. Even if one cannot see inside the buildings, however, the sites themselves are usually accessible and may still be visited.

It is impossible in this handbook to describe every literary and film location or site otherwise associated with James Bond or his creator. Instead, this guide presents a selection of sites that are significant, familiar, little known, quirky, or surprising. In many ways, the book represents my own journey through Bond's Britain and reflects my interests in history, archaeology, and cuisine. Whether you are dipping in to discover sites with Bond connections in your area, or are planning a tour of Bond locations, or you simply want to use it as a companion while discovering the Bond books and films, to paraphrase Tim Rice's words for the title theme to OCTOPUSSY, sung by Rita Coolidge, I hope it provides a sweet distraction for an hour or two.

This way to explore James Bond's Britain!

LONDON, CITY OF WESTMINSTER

St Sophia's Greek Orthodox Cathedral, Moscow Road, W2 4LQ
www.stsophia.org.uk

Having discovered in St Petersburg that fellow computer programmer Boris Grishenko (Alan Cumming) appears to be, apart from herself, the only survivor from the explosion at Russia's Severnaya space weapons research establishment in GOLDENEYE, Natalya Simonova (Izabella Scorupco) arranges to meet him at a nearby church. It is a trap, and after she arrives, Simonova is greeted not only by Grishenko, but renegade Russian general Ourumov (Gottfried John) and Janus henchwoman Xenia Onatopp (Famke Janssen).

The interior scenes were filmed at the magnificent St Sophia's Greek Orthodox Cathedral in London, a Byzantine-inspired, yellow and red brick structure with stone dressings and a copper-clad domed roof built in 1878–79. We see two areas of the church in the film: the rectangular porch or narthex that separates the front entrance of the church from the main prayer hall, and the main prayer hall itself. The narthex, where Simonova is unceremoniously grabbed by Grishenko, is paved in marble and ornately decorated with wall mosaics and stencilling on the ceiling and appears today as it did in the film. The main prayer hall, which is accessed through a curtained entrance from the narthex, is in the form of a Greek cross in plan and comprises a nave, transepts, and a sanctuary. As Simonova enters the hall before meeting Grishenko, she takes in the splendour of the domed roof – depicting Christ seated on a rainbow with the earth by his feet – and, suspended from the roof, the large, silver-plated double Greek cross with ruby lamps. Again, the space is unchanged since its appearance on the big screen.

The cathedral is open to the public during the week, except on Mondays and Thursdays. Do check its website for opening times. Visitors are welcome to walk around the church or sit and reflect – but keep an eye out for Boris Grishenko.

St Sophia's Greek Orthodox Cathedral, as seen in GOLDENEYE.

Queen Mary's Rose Garden, Inner Circle, The Regent's Park, NW1 4PA
www.royalparks.org.uk

Suffering with what Secret Service medical consultant Sir James Moloney diagnoses as shock and neurosis but what we would now recognise as depression, James Bond spends a late August lunchtime in *You Only Live Twice* sitting on a bench in Queen Mary's Rose Garden in Regent's Park thinking about his health, the oppressive summer heat, bee corpses, and his late wife, Tracy, who died at arch-villain Blofeld's hands eight months earlier. As a place of contemplation, the

***Queen Mary's Rose Garden, Regent's Park, where Bond takes time to reflect in* You Only Live Twice.**

rose garden cannot be equalled. In the summer, it is a riot of colour and fragrance and filled with the drowsy hum of bees and people alike. The circular garden is set within the larger Queen Mary's Garden inside the park's Inner Circle. The park is easily reached by public transport, the nearest Underground stations being Regent's Park and Baker Street.

Marble Arch, W1H 7EJ

As revealed in *Live and Let Die* and *Thunderball*, among other stories, Bond's commute from his flat off the King's Road in Chelsea to his office in a tall, grim building overlooking Regent's Park involves his driving – 007 rarely catches the tube and never the bus – east along the King's Road, north on Sloane Street, and into Hyde Park, exiting at Marble Arch. From there Bond takes a round-the-houses route to Baker Street before reaching the southern edge of Regent's Park. During his drive to the office in *On Her Majesty's Secret Service*, his Syncraphone – a paging system that is introduced by the Secret Service to be carried by all officers – begins bleeping, requiring Bond to stop as soon as he has found a telephone and call in. At this moment, Bond is in Hyde Park. He accelerates out of the park and stops at a public telephone box at

Marble Arch. At the time the novel was published in 1963, there was an array of telephone boxes west of Marble Arch at the edge of Hyde Park and the junction of Bayswater Road and Edgware Road, and judging by his route, it is plausible that Bond stops there to make his call.

27 Green Street, W1K 7AZ

Ian Fleming was born at 27 Green Street, the London home of his parents, Evelyn and Valentine Fleming, on 28 May 1908. The red-brick townhouse, like most of the properties on the north side of the street, was built in the late Victorian/early Edwardian period, although the street has its origins in the mid-eighteenth century. Over the decades, the street has attracted a number of notable residents, among them the poet William Blake, who lived at number 23 in the 1780s, the Beatles, who shared a flat at number 57 in 1963, and fashion designer Alexander McQueen, who lived at number 7.

Dorchester Hotel, 53 Park Lane, W1K 1QA

www.dorchestercollection.com

The world-renowned Dorchester Hotel is a must-visit location for any Bond lover, boasting, as it can, of connections with both the literary and cinematic 007. Two actors were revealed to the world as the new James Bond at a press conference at the hotel – George Lazenby on 7 October 1968, and Roger Moore on 1 August 1972 – and the producers of the Bond films, Harry Saltzman and Cubby Broccoli,

Ian Fleming's birthplace: 27 Green Street, London.

often stayed at the Dorchester, or they would hold meetings or entertain there. In William Boyd's 2013 Bond novel, *Solo*, 007 stays at the hotel. The novel begins with Bond waking up in his room, and, after showering and dressing, he goes down to the dining room for breakfast (four scrambled eggs, with six rashers of unsmoked back bacon on the side and accompanied by strong black coffee). The hotel also boasts the Vesper Bar, a cocktail bar named after the drink that Ian Fleming created for *Casino Royale* and, since the 2006 film version of the novel, has become a standard on bar menus the world over.

Morland and Co. (former site of), 83 Grosvenor Street, W1K 3JZ

Like his creator, Ian Fleming, Bond has quite a smoking habit. When he is on the job and working through the day and long into the night, as he does at the casino in the northern French coastal resort of Royale-les-Eaux in *Casino Royale*, he might smoke up to seventy cigarettes a day. Even off the clock, his normal daily consumption approaches sixty; he admits to Solitaire in *Live and Let Die* that he usually gets through three packs a day. Bond is undoubtedly a very favoured customer of Morlands of Grosvenor Street, who not only supply his cigarettes, but prepare a special blend of Balkan and Turkish tobacco and mark the cigarettes with three gold bands. The gold bands allude to Bond's naval rank of commander, although

The site of Morlands (central building), tobacconist to Ian Fleming and James Bond.

curiously, in *Thunderball*, he reveals that he has been smoking the special cigarettes since his teens.

Bond's choice of cigarette, and his copious consumption, reflects Fleming's own smoking habits. Morlands did indeed exist and had premises at 83 Grosvenor Street. Today, at that address you will find a thin, white-fronted building sandwiched between the red-brick number 84 and number 80, a brown corner building.

EON House, 138 Piccadilly, W1J 7NR

The headquarters of EON Productions, the film company led by Barbara Broccoli and Michael G. Wilson and, until 2025, responsible for creating, and maintaining, one of the most successful film series in the world, can be found at the west end of Piccadilly in a discreet town house – built in the late eighteenth century and remodelled in the late nineteenth century – next to a branch of the Hard Rock Café. A company nameplate on the wall provides the only clue that Bond's fate was plotted and steered within its walls. Originally, under the leadership of its founders Albert R. Broccoli and Harry Saltzman, EON Productions were based at 2 South Audley Street (W1K 1HF), also in Mayfair.

The London office of EON Productions.

The May Fair, Stratton Street, W1J 8LT

www.radissonhotels.com

In the lesser-known short story, '007 in New York', which remained unpublished in Britain until 1999 and is now included as part of the *Octopussy* collection, we learn that Bond had a particular recipe for scrambled eggs, which he had instructed the kitchen staff of New York's Plaza Hotel to make on a previous visit. The recipe for 'Scrambled eggs "James Bond"' was given in full as a footnote to the story.

The story, along with the recipe, was first published in the *Sunday Herald Tribune* in September 1963, but the recipe had an earlier appearance, having previously been published in 1961 in a collection of favourite recipes of the famous, *Celebrity Cooking for You*. This, however, was not the first time that the

The May Fair, the home of scrambled eggs 'James Bond'.

recipe had appeared in print. Fleming's 'Atticus' column of 25 December 1955 in the *Sunday Times* included a small piece about scrambled eggs under the heading 'Oeufs Attique' in which Fleming reproduced the recipe for scrambled eggs by one Bartolemo Calderoni, chef at the May Fair hotel. Thus, 'Scrambled eggs "James Bond"' is really 'Scrambled eggs "Bartolemo Calderoni"'.

The Ritz London, 150 Piccadilly, St James's, W1J 9BR
www.theritzlondon.com

When Bond stays at the ultra-luxurious Ritz hotel in London, he is usually not quite himself. In *Diamonds Are Forever*, assuming the identity of diamond smuggler Peter Franks, 007 is told by Tiffany Case to stay at the Ritz and use the address for immigration purposes. The following day, he is collected from the Piccadilly entrance of the hotel and taken to London airport (Heathrow) to continue his journey along the diamond smuggling pipeline. In *The Man with the Golden Gun*, Bond stays at the Ritz, having returned to England from Russia, where he has been brainwashed by Colonel Boris. The Ritz accords with how Colonel Boris views Bond's high-living lifestyle, but the effect, along with the clothes and accessories, is something of a parody of 007's habits and preferences. In the novel, Bond exits the hotel through the Arlington Street entrance just off Piccadilly.

The Arlington Street entrance of the Ritz Hotel, London.

Scott's (site of), 2 Coventry Street, W1D 7DH
scotts-mayfair.com

At one point during the events of *Moonraker*, Bond is sitting in a restaurant, waiting for Gala Brand to arrive, at a table on the first floor that overlooks Piccadilly Circus and the Haymarket. The restaurant is unnamed, but the description identifies it as Scott's on the corner of Coventry Street and Great Windmill Street. The seafood restaurant and oyster bar is a favourite of Bond's. In *Diamonds Are Forever*, 007 treats chief-of-staff Bill Tanner to lunch at Scott's, tempting him with dressed crab and a pint of black velvet. Ian Fleming was a regular visitor to Scott's as well, and he listed it among his favourite restaurants in an article entitled 'London's Best Dining', published in the US magazine *Holiday* in 1956. In 1967, the restaurant

The site of Bond's favourite restaurant, Scott's, which is now a Five Guys restaurant.

moved to Mount Street in Mayfair, but Bond lovers can still dine at its former location, being home to a Five Guys burger restaurant. Before entering the restaurant, look out for the 'S' monogram, scallop shell and fish carvings on the Bath stone frontage of the late nineteenth-century building. Once you have ordered your food from the serving counter, do follow Bond and go up to the first floor to eat. Window seats, however, are no longer available.

For a more authentic Bondian experience, a visit to Scott's on Mount Street is recommended. The menu there includes several dishes that Bond has eaten in the course of his adventures, including Dover sole, grilled lobster, oysters, ray wing, caviar, and, of course, dressed crab. Black velvet is off the menu (you need to go to Rules for that), but the Vesper Martini, introduced in *Casino Royale*, is on offer.

Sotheby's, 34–35 New Bond Street, W1A 2AA
www.sothebys.com

It is a marvellous piece of sleight of hand. Bond (Roger Moore) beckons the assistant in the saleroom of Sotheby's, takes from the proffered cushion what is described by the auctioneer (Philip Voss) as a superb green-gold Imperial Easter egg by Carl Fabergé, switches it for a fake egg behind his sale catalogue, and places the fake on to the cushion. The film is OCTOPUSSY, and Bond is at the auction house to discover who is selling the egg – suspected to be a means by the Soviets to raise funds – and who is buying. After the auction, 007 stands by a newspaper kiosk outside Sotheby's New Bond Street entrance and signals an MI6 agent in a black cab to follow the purchaser of the egg, one Kamal Khan (Louis Jourdan). The kiosk has since gone, but the entrance to Sotheby's is unchanged from how it appeared in the film. The building was built in the early eighteenth century

The New Bond Street entrance of Sotheby's.

but was altered in the mid-nineteenth century when Sotheby's moved in. The auction house once again served as a Bondian location when it provided the backdrop for pivotal sequences in Kim Sherwood's second 'Double O' novel, *A Spy Like Me*.

Sotheby's (SI2 Gallery), 31, 33 St George Street, W1S 2FL

The Sotheby's auction sequence in OCTOPUSSY is taken from Ian Fleming's short story 'The Property of a Lady', published in the *Octopussy and The Living Daylights* collection. There are some differences between them, however. Notably, the Fabergé item for sale in the short story is not an imperial Easter egg (although Easter eggs are mentioned), but a terrestrial globe. And Bond does not use the New Bond Street entrance, but Sotheby's St George Street entrance, today known as the SI2 Gallery. In the saleroom, 007 spots the Soviet agent tasked with raising the price of the piece and follows him back out the St George Street entrance and into Conduit Street just metres away.

The terrestrial globe that is the focus of the story is a fictional piece based on two separate works. One of them is an Easter egg in the form of a clock, which was never produced, but exists as a watercolour design, and the other a miniature terrestrial globe. Both items are described in the seminal volume by Fabergé expert Kenneth Snowman, *The Art of Carl Fabergé*, published in 1962.

The George Street entrance of Sotheby's.

Sotheby's

To acknowledge Kenneth Snowman's help in Fleming's research, the art expert himself appears as a character in the story, which was first published in 1963 in Sotheby's yearbook, *The Ivory Hammer*. Snowman's volume was also a sourcebook for Richard Maibaum and George MacDonald Fraser, the screenwriters of OCTOPUSSY. During his briefing with M (Robert Brown), and with art expert Jim Fanning (Douglas Wilmer) in attendance, Bond is handed an auction catalogue, which is turned to the page on which the film's imperial Easter egg is described. The text in the catalogue entry is taken almost verbatim from the entry for the Coronation Egg in Snowman's volume, indicating that this egg, made for the Tsarina Feodorovna in 1897, inspired the prop egg we see in the film.

Wartski (site of), 138 Regent Street, W1B 5SG

Bond visits Wartski, jeweller to the royal houses of Europe, in Regent Street in the short story 'The Property of a Lady'. He is there to consult Kenneth Snowman, chairman of Wartski and an expert in the work of Carl Fabergé, about the sale at Sotheby's of a terrestrial globe, described in the story

The former site on Regent's Street of Wartski, purveyors of fine jewellery, now occupied by Tommy Hilfiger.

as a very important globe designed by Fabergé in 1917. Bond is admitted into the showroom and marvels at the gold and diamond pieces on display. Wartski is now at 60 St James Street, SW1 1LE, and its chairmanship has passed through the generations. Today it is run by Hector Snowman, grandson of Kenneth. The Regent Street premises is now occupied by Tommy Hilfiger.

Rules, 34–35 Maiden Lane, WC2E 7LB
rules.co.uk

In SPECTRE, M (Ralph Fiennes) is having supper at Rules restaurant in Covent Garden when Moneypenny (Naomie Harris) and Q (Ben Whishaw) come in with some important information about the mysterious Franz Oberhauser. The original script had M dine at a small, discreet Italian restaurant, but the film-makers in the end opted for Rules, purported to be London's oldest restaurant.

The position of M's table at the back of the restaurant is unchanged since the film, giving diners the opportunity to dine like Bond's chief. Booking in advance is recommended, and while it is possible to request 'M's table', being seated there is not

Rules Restaurant, where M has supper in SPECTRE.

guaranteed, especially for single diners or couples, as parties of four take priority. Wherever one sits, however, one can still enjoy the comfortable surroundings, the impeccable service, and the sublime menu, which offers traditional British cuisine, with such treats as oysters, salmon, crab, pies, steak and kidney puddings, and game.

Malaysia House, 57 Trafalgar Square, St James's, WC2N 5DU

In THE LIVING DAYLIGHTS, MI6 is located at the south side of Trafalgar Square, next to Admiralty Arch. A sign for MI6 cover organisation Universal Exports is placed above the door at the rounded corner of what is now Malaysia House, home to the Malaysia Tourism Promotion Board. The building can be seen again, albeit in the background, when James Bond (Daniel Craig), Madeleine Swann (Léa Seydoux), Tanner (Rory Kinnear), and M (Ralph Fiennes) exit the MI6 safe house in Spring Gardens in SPECTRE.

The National Gallery, Trafalgar Square, WC2N 5DN

www.nationalgallery.org.uk

When gadget-master Q was reintroduced to the film series after a two-film hiatus in SKYFALL, the film-makers eschewed the usual sequence of organised chaos in Q's workshop, with technicians in lab coats running around in the background, gadgets being tested and invariably failing, and Q in the centre,

Malaysia House, once the fictional location of the British Secret Service.

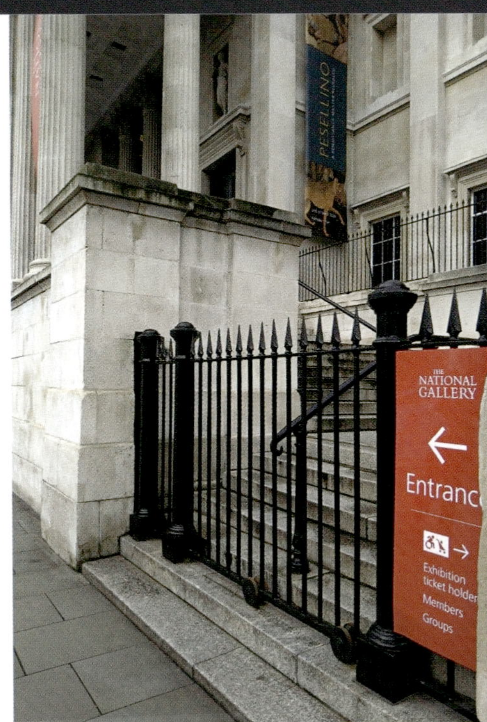

In SKYFALL, Bond enters the National Gallery via the steps of the front portico.

somehow in control and finding time not only to equip James Bond, but also bemoan Bond's casual attitude to his gadgets. Instead, Bond (Daniel Craig) meets Q (Ben Whishaw) in the quiet, sparse, and reflective space of the National Gallery. Before them is J.M.W. Turner's 1838 painting, 'The Fighting Temeraire', depicting an old warship being taken away to be broken up. (In a nice coincidence, Ian Fleming's mother, Eve, lived for a while at Turner's former home in Chelsea.) The choice of painting is symbolic of Bond and his changing world, and the scene serves to reset – and rebalance – the relationship between Bond and Q. The painting remains on display in room 34 of the National Gallery, and visitors, like Bond, can sit in front of it and think about what they see. In the film, 007 enters the gallery via the front entrance within the columned portico on the north side of Trafalgar Square. It is no longer possible to enter this way, although Bond lovers may follow his route as far as the steps flanking the eastern side of the portico. Visitors must then enter the gallery via the Salisbury Wing to the west of the main building.

Charing Cross Station, Strand, WC2N 5HS

Charing Cross Station plays a small but important role in the diamond smuggling pipeline that Bond is preparing to smash in *Diamonds Are Forever*. When she needs to call her contact, the mysterious ABC, Tiffany Case leaves her room at the (fictional) Trafalgar Palace, walks across Trafalgar Square and into Charing Cross Station. Once there, she goes to her usual callbox and makes her call. There are, perhaps surprisingly, still public telephones at Charing Cross: at the Trafalgar Square exit near the left

The main entrance of Charing Cross Station.

luggage facilities and in the central exit to the Strand. If ever you are in Central London and need to call ABC – a minicab firm, a pizza parlour, or perhaps even the eighties pop band – for that extra Bondian touch, you might like to follow Case's path into the station and make your call from a payphone there.

Charing Cross Underground Station, Northumberland Avenue, WC2N 5DE

After causing mayhem on the London Underground in SKYFALL, Raoul Silva (Javier Bardem), disguised as a police officer, exits the Underground close to the south entrance of Embankment station on Northumberland Avenue.

The Northumberland Avenue entrance of Charing Cross Underground Station, seen briefly in SKYFALL.

Silva looks on as police officers manage the crowd of people congregating around the entrance, a semicircular structure located between the Playhouse Theatre and the Embankment Place tunnel. In the film, the entrance is identified as Embankment station, but today the entrance provides access to Charing Cross station between certain hours.

Brooks's, St James's Street, SW1A 1LN
www.brooksclub.org

In *Moonraker*, with his mind on the task ahead of him – to determine how Sir Hugo Drax cheats at cards and to defeat him in a game of bridge in the sumptuous rooms at Blades, a gentleman's club located in Park Place (incorrectly identified by Ian Fleming as Park Street) – Bond leaves his Bentley outside Brooks's Club on the corner of St James Street and Park Place and walks round to Blades.

In common with the fictional club of Blades, Brooks's was established in the second half of the eighteenth century. Both also appear to have been designed in neo-classical style. Brooks's was built in 1778 after a design by architect Henry Holland. In *Moonraker*, Fleming notes the Adam frontage of Blades, which identifies the architect

Brooks's on St James's Street, with M's club, Blades, round the corner on Park Place.

as Robert Adam, who was responsible for, among many other architectural triumphs, the Bond-related location of Luton Hoo. We can imagine, therefore, that 007 enters the club through an impressive entrance built in dressed stone blocks and complete with Greek- or Roman-style columns, cornices, friezes, and pediments.

Later in the novel, Bond parks outside another club, Boodle's, which is located on St James's Street opposite Brooks's. Parking at either club provides good views of Park Place. Blades does not exist, of course, but one can still follow Bond's footsteps and turn the corner into the little street.

The Reform Club, 104 Pall Mall, St James's, SW1Y 5EW
www.reformclub.com

The front door of the Reform Club, which stood in for Blades in DIE ANOTHER DAY.

That Neal Purvis and Robert Wade, the screenwriters of DIE ANOTHER DAY, took their inspiration for the plot of the film from Ian Fleming's *Moonraker* is evident from the Sir Hugo Drax-like character of the principal villain, Sir Gustav Graves (Toby Stephens), an early draft of the script that included a character called Gala Brand (later renamed Miranda Frost, played by Rosamund Pike), and a sequence involving fencing bouts and equally painful puns at Blades club. The interiors for the scenes at Blades were filmed at the Reform Club on Pall Mall, the institution immortalised in Jules Verne's *Around the World in Eighty Days*. The club offers its members a programme of music evenings, guest speakers, black-tie dinners, drinks receptions and so on, but not normally, it seems, fencing. Access is reserved to members only, but non-members can at least pose outside its front door.

Carlton Hotel (site of), New Zealand House, 80 Haymarket, St James's, SW1Y 4TE

The New Zealand High Commission at New Zealand House occupies the former site of the Carlton Hotel. It was at the hotel's restaurant, the Carlton Grill on 24 May 1939, that, over lunch with Director of Naval Intelligence (DNI) Admiral Godfrey and two others, including former deputy DNI Sir Aubrey Hugh Smith, Ian Fleming was recruited to the Naval Intelligence Department, becoming assistant to Admiral Godfrey. The importance of this moment in James Bond lore cannot be overstated. Fleming would draw on many of his experiences and encounters in naval intelligence during the Second World War when he came to create the character of James Bond and think up his improbable, but not impossible, plots for the 007 stories. The Carlton Hotel, where Fleming briefly resided at the start of the war, was destroyed by bombing in 1940. After the war, the site was cleared, with New Zealand House being built there between 1959 and 1963.

Dukes Bar, 35 St James's Place, St James's, SW1A 1NY
dukeshotel.com

Dukes Bar, located within Dukes Hotel, was one of Ian Fleming's regular haunts. It is famous for its Martinis,

The site of the Carlton Hotel, where Ian Fleming was recruited to Naval Intelligence.

Dukes Bar, the home of the martini, shaken, not stirred.

and it is said to have inspired the way that Bond's Martinis are prepared, these being shaken, not stirred. A visit to Dukes, where one sinks into rich armchairs and drinks are made at your table, is an experience that is second to none. Various Martinis, including the Vesper, are on the menu. There is no need to book, but during busy times you may have to wait for a table.

New Scotland Yard (site of), Norman Shaw Buildings, 1 Victoria Embankment (South Building)/A3211, SW1A 2HZ (North Building)

Bond becomes quite familiar with the courtyards and corridors of New Scotland Yard over the course of his adventures. In *Moonraker*, he pays a visit to the Yard on Victoria Embankment to discuss with Commissioner Vallance the practicalities of taking on the role of security officer at Sir Hugo Drax's Moonraker establishment, and to smooth any friction between the Special Branch and MI6. In *Diamonds Are Forever*, 007 has another appointment with Commissioner Vallance, this time to be briefed further on the diamond smuggling network and to discuss Special Branch's role in the operation to penetrate the pipeline.

Between 1890 and 1967, New Scotland Yard was located along Victoria Embankment in a pair of buildings constructed in red brick with Portland stone bands on a granite base. Both are now known as the Norman Shaw Buildings, named after the architect Richard Norman Shaw. He gave the buildings a defensive, castle-like appearance by adding turrets to the corners and arranging the wings of the north building around a central courtyard. In *Moonraker*, Fleming notes that Bond looks out from a window into the courtyard below, which places him in the north building. As if acknowledging Norman Shaw's intentions, Bond reflects that the building reminds him of a prison.

The Norman Shaw Buildings, the former site of New Scotland Yard.

The Spy Bar, 57 Whitehall, SW1A 2BX
theowo.london/the-spy-bar

The Old War Office, whose exterior was seen on screen in the establishing shot of MI6 headquarters in OCTOPUSSY, A VIEW TO A KILL, and LICENCE TO KILL, and whose interior was used as headquarters in SKYFALL, has been transformed into Raffles, a five-star hotel. In the basement of the hotel is the Spy Bar, a drinking den with an espionage theme and plenty of nods to James Bond.

Whitehall Court, SW1A 2EP
Bond has no worries about parking in central London. When 007 (Daniel Craig) is persuaded to return to MI6 after retiring to Jamaica in NO TIME TO DIE, he arrives in style, sweeping into a space outside number 4 Whitehall Court in his vintage Aston Martin V8 (Bond's car in THE LIVING DAYLIGHTS). Clearly, the prospect of a parking fine does not bother him, as, having stopped on double yellow lines, he nonchalantly adjusts his cuffs and strides like a panther into the north entrance of the Ministry of Defence opposite Whitehall Court. Given his fondness for France, the literary Bond may have taken a little time to admire the architecture of Whitehall Court, which was built in 1884 in Portland stone in a style inspired by the châteaux of the Loire valley.

Whitehall Court provides a convenient parking spot for James Bond in NO TIME TO DIE.

27 Spring Gardens, SW1A 2BA

The entrance to an MI6 safe house in SPECTRE – named Hildebrand after Ian Fleming's short story 'The Hildebrand Rarity' – is located in Spring Gardens, a lane off Trafalgar Square and immediately to the east of Admiralty Arch. Bond (Daniel Craig), Madeleine Swann (Léa Seydoux), Tanner (Rory Kinnear), and M (Ralph Fiennes) step through one of the distinctive grille doors of number 27 and turn towards Trafalgar Square (note Malaysia House in the background, which doubled for MI6 headquarters in THE LIVING DAYLIGHTS). Actually, not everyone heads that way. Deciding that Bond's world is not for her, Swann turns away from him and walks further into Spring Gardens. As this leads to a dead end, she presumably turns down the short lane that connects Spring Gardens with the Mall. (Note that the postcode given above is for 35 Spring Gardens, as a postcode for number 27 does not exist or is not available. Well, it *is* a safehouse after all!)

Spring Gardens, the site of the MI6 safe house in SPECTRE.

The Mall, St James's, SW1Y 5AH

Part of Madeleine Swann's (Léa Seydoux) walking route to her London office is revealed in NO TIME TO DIE, when she is seen crossing the Mall at the junction with Horse Guards Road, with the Royal Artillery Boer War Memorial on the edge of St James's Park in the background. She heads towards the steps that take her to Carlton House Terrace, where presumably her psychiatry practice is located.

Duck Island, 69 Horse Guards Road, SW1A 2BJ

His Kentish adventure concluded, having foiled Sir Hugo Drax's plans to drop an atomic bomb on London in *Moonraker*, Bond is looking forward to spending time driving through France with Special Branch agent Gala Brand. Bond has arranged to meet Brand at an area of seating facing Duck Island on St James's Park Lake, and has walked there, presumably through the park, from the junction of Queen Anne's Gate

Duck Island on St James's Park Lake, where Bond awaits the arrival of Gala Brand in **Moonraker.**

and Birdcage Walk on the south side of the park. Alas for James, Gala has other plans. As she arrives, her fiancé, a Detective Inspector Vivian, waits discreetly a short distance away.

There are benches between St James's Park Lake and Horse Guards Parade at the east end of the park where Bond appears to have waited, providing an opportunity for 007 lovers to recreate his meeting or arrange their own special rendezvous.

22B Ebury Street, SW1W 0LU

While working as a stockbroker in the City of London, Ian Fleming lived around the corner from Victoria Station at 22B Ebury Street between 1936 and 1939. There, he led the carefree bachelor life, entertaining women and hosting dinner and card-playing evenings for his friends. Consisting of five bays, the central three bays taking the form of a classical Greek temple, complete with Doric columns, triglyph frieze and pediment, number 22 is one of the most distinctive buildings in the area. It was built in 1830 by J.P. Gandy-Deering to accommodate the Pimlico Literary Institute, a non-conformist school intended, as the Latin inscription above the door records, to

22B Ebury Street: Ian Fleming's home and literary inspiration.

instruct 'boys in Christ's faith and moral and literary arts'. In the 1930s, the then owners, the Grosvenor Estate, divided the building into four apartments, and number 22B was leased to the leader of the British Union of Fascists, Oswald Mosley. He subsequently sold his lease to Fleming, whose residency is today commemorated by a blue plaque.

In *Moonraker*, Fleming makes Ebury Street the London home of villain Sir Hugo Drax (who, readers learn, had moved there from Grosvenor Square). Whether Fleming had his own former home in mind is not clear, but we do know that it is situated at the Buckingham Palace end of Ebury Street, which could include number 22 or be further along in part of the road that has since become Beeston Place. However, the house does make a literary appearance, albeit in a different thriller. In *Eye for an Eye* (1900), a mystery novel by one of Fleming's favourite authors, William Le Queux, a mysterious man suspected of murder is followed by a detective from Victoria Station into Ebury Street and is seen ducking into, of all places, number 22.

16 Victoria Square, SW1W 0RA

Ian Fleming's final London residence was in Victoria Square, just off Buckingham Palace Road. It was an address that saw the birth and growing success of Fleming's creation, James Bond; the author lived here from 1953 until his death in 1964.

61 Horseferry Road, SW1P 2ED

Where does the Bond of the film series live? During the tenure of Pierce Brosnan and for much of Daniel Craig's time as 007, his home address was given on prop passports as 61 Horseferry Road, Westminster. There have been occasional variations; an Avis car rental agreement produced for TOMORROW NEVER DIES misspelled the first line of Bond's address as 61 Horsen Ferry Road and gave the postcode as S1, but essentially the same address has been used for some years through different lead actors and changes in prop department staff. Bond lovers, however, will have trouble locating the property, as it does not in fact exist. The closest visitors can get to Bond's home is 65 Horseferry Road, which is the Westminster Coroner's Court.

REST OF LONDON

BARNET

Brent Cross Shopping Centre Car Park, Prince Charles Drive, Brent Cross, NW4 3FP
Brent Cross Shopping Centre has at least two claims to fame. One is that it was Britain's first out-of-town shopping centre, opening its doors in 1976. The second is that its multistorey car park, standing in for the car park of the Hotel Atlantic Kempinski in Hamburg, provided the location for a thrilling sequence in TOMORROW NEVER DIES in which Bond (Pierce Brosnan) remotely steers his BMW 750iL up successive levels to evade Elliot Carver's goons. The location remains the principal parking area for shopping centre customers, and, amazingly, there is no charge for leaving one's car.

CITY OF LONDON

Mitre Court Chambers, 4 Old Mitre Court, EC4Y 7BP
Ian Fleming maintained an office at Mitre Court in the heart of his journalistic stomping ground in Fleet Street (he had a

Ian Fleming maintained an office at Mitre Court, off Fleet Street.

long association with the *Sunday Times*, serving as its Foreign Manager, 'Atticus' columnist, and special correspondent). It was in his office here that Fleming corrected the manuscripts of his Bond novels and dealt with 007-related correspondence and business.

Frobisher Crescent, Silk Street, EC2Y 8DS
www.barbican.org.uk

Frobisher Crescent, part of the Barbican estate, played host to the world of James Bond when it doubled as an MI6-run building in QUANTUM OF SOLACE. In the film, we see M (Judi Dench) and Tanner (Rory Kinnear) walking across the centre's semicircular courtyard in conversation, over the phone, with Bond (Daniel Craig).

College of Arms, 130 Queen Victoria Street, EC4V 4BT
www.college-of-arms.gov.uk

The principal roles of the College of Arms are to grant coats of arms, investigate rights to existing ones, and undertake genealogical research on behalf of the United Kingdom and the Commonwealth. To Bond lovers, however, it is best known as a location in both the book

Frobisher Crescent, near the Barbican Centre, doubled for MI6 headquarters in QUANTUM OF SOLACE.

and the film of *On Her Majesty's Secret Service*. Bond visits the college to learn about arch-villain Ernst Stavro Blofeld's request for its services to support his claim to the title of Count Balthazar de Bleuchamp, or Comte Balthazar de Bleuville, as it is in the book.

In ON HER MAJESTY'S SECRET SERVICE, we are introduced to the college by means of an exterior shot of the front of the building, which is on Queen Victoria Street; 007 (George Lazenby) arrives in his Aston Martin DB5 and parks in the courtyard. This scene was shot on location and the building today is little changed. The film cuts to an interior view of a hall, where Bond meets a porter in a cherry-red uniform, a uniform that was accurate at the time and is still worn today. The porter takes him through a side door to the office of one of the heralds, Sir Hilary Bray (George Baker), who goes by the impressive title of Sable Basilisk. The hall is in fact the Earl Marshal's Court, which may still, in theory, sit in order to hear and resolve heraldic disputes. The court in the film is a studio recreation, but apart from being larger and having more doors, it is a fair depiction of the real thing. The throne, enclosing rail, wall panelling, portraits, and flags present in the actual

***The grand entrance to the College of Arms, which featured in both the novel and film of* On Her Majesty's Secret Service.**

court are all as represented on screen. The attention to detail is such that the screen court even depicts the crests and other devices above the doors and the radiators along the wall. In the film, Sable Basilisk's door is suitably ornate, again an accurate depiction, as all the heralds' office doors are rather elaborate; the office of Portcullis, for example, has a golden portcullis within a carved rosette-type device above the door.

Today, the College of Arms is open to public enquiries and tours are occasionally given. The Bond connection is very much kept alive. A few pages of the original film script are on display in a corner of the court room, and Bond-related books are available to purchase from the receptionist.

Bank Station, Princes Street, EC3V 3LA; Bank of England Museum, Bartholomew Lane, EC2R 8AH
www.bankofengland.co.uk

It is difficult to imagine Bond jostling with commuters and tourists on the London Underground, yet he occasionally does so. In SKYFALL, 007 (Daniel Craig) pursues Raoul Silva (Javier Bardem) through the crowded Underground network (filming of the station scenes took place on the walkways and platform on the disused Jubilee Line connection at Charing Cross Station), and in *Goldfinger* he heads down into Bank Station after a meeting with Colonel Smithers of the Bank of England's research department.

The Bank of England, which Bond visits in **Goldfinger.**

While at the bank, Bond tells Smithers (this in 1959) that he thinks the old £5 note was the most beautiful money in the world. It was a view shared by Ian Fleming himself, who had expressed the same opinion in an 'Atticus' column in the *Sunday Times* in 1954. Are they correct? Do visit the Bank of England Museum, which holds a comprehensive collection of bank notes, and judge for yourself.

10 Trinity Square, EC3N 4AJ

When, in SKYFALL, M (Judi Dench) and Tanner (Rory Kinnear) arrive by car at the parliamentary hearing that is examining MI6's handling of the loss of the stolen hard drive containing identities of agents across the world, they pull up at the columned entrance of 10 Trinity Square, a grand building designed by Sir Edwin Cooper and built between 1912 and 1922 for the Port of London Authority. It is now home to the Four Seasons Hotel London.

10 Trinity Square, which made an appearance in SKYFALL.

GREENWICH

The O2, Peninsula Square, SE10 0DX
www.theo2.co.uk

The denouement of the high-speed boat chase in the pre-titles sequence of THE WORLD IS NOT ENOUGH takes place at the O2 arena (originally known as the Millennium Dome) on the south bank of the Thames. The assassin known as the Cigar Girl (Maria Grazia Cucinotta) brings her Sunseeker Superhawk boat to a rapid halt in front of the arena, leaps out, and hijacks a hot-air balloon. As the Cigar Girl ascends, Bond (Pierce Brosnan) uses the Sunseeker as a ramp to lift his jet-powered 'Q Boat' into the air, allowing him to catch hold of the balloon's mooring ropes. Before they can go very much further, a shot causes the balloon to explode and, in the nick of time, Bond lets go of the rope and falls on to the roof of the arena, his slide down it being arrested by another set of ropes.

The O2 is an entertainment venue comprising a vast arena, designer shopping, a cinema, and bars and

The O2 arena, where the pre-titles sequence of THE WORLD IS NOT ENOUGH comes to a dramatic conclusion.

restaurants, all under one dome-shaped roof. It also offers outdoor, rooftop climbing, which gives Bond lovers an opportunity to follow in the footsteps of 007 but without the perilous sliding. There is ample parking at the venue, and it is easily reached by public transport (the nearest Underground station being North Greenwich), including boat; Uber Boats by Thames Clippers operate a river service to the dome.

HAMMERSMITH

Furnivall Sculling Club, 19 Lower Mall, W6 9DJ

Following angry words in M's office in NO TIME TO DIE, Bond (Daniel Craig) and M (Ralph Fiennes) have a calmer exchange of views on the bank of the River Thames within sight of Hammersmith Bridge about the Heracles project and the terrible implications of the technology getting into the wrong hands. The two meet

Bond and M have a few minutes of conversation opposite the Furnivall Sculling Club in NO TIME TO DIE.

on Lower Mall at the corner of an alcove opposite the Furnivall Sculling Club. (Sharp-eyed viewers will spot a quad sculling boat on the river in the background.) The wall against which M is leaning can be identified by the white marks on the corner. The alcove is where the rowing crews gain access to the river, so if you are recreating the scene, do watch out for boats being manoeuvred into and out of the water.

KENSINGTON AND CHELSEA

1 Stanley Gardens, W11 2ND

Seeing Bond's (Daniel Craig) sparsely decorated flat in SPECTRE, Moneypenny (Naomie Harris) wonders if he has just moved in. The exterior of 007's first-floor flat was filmed at 1 Stanley Gardens in Notting Hill. There is no indication in the film that the location is intended to represent Bond's Horseferry Road residence, the address

1 Stanley Gardens, Bond's home on the big screen.

that has traditionally been placed on Bond's prop passports, but it is in keeping with the literary Bond, whose Wellington Square residence is within walking distance of Stanley Gardens. Slightly confusingly, the front door of 1 Stanley Gardens is situated in Stanley Cresent.

82 Cadogan Square, SW1X 0EA

Audiences are treated to a rare view of the private residence of M (Judi Dench) in SKYFALL. Arriving home on a miserable, rain-soaked evening, M finds Bond (Daniel Craig) in her sitting room, reporting back for duty in a manner that can be described as most irregular. So much for M's instruction to Bond in CASINO ROYALE never to break into her home again. Exterior shots of M arriving at her house were filmed outside number 82 Cadogan Square. This is not the location's only Bond connection. The property was once home to Bond film composer John Barry. Another resident of the square was Francisco Scaramanga himself, Christopher Lee.

82 Cadogan Square, the home of M.

30 Wellington Square, SW3 4NR

When locating Bond's literary London home, Ian Fleming kept the details vague. What we do know, from *Moonraker*, *From Russia With Love*, and *Thunderball*, is that 007 lives in a flat in a converted Regency house in a little square with plane trees off the King's Road in Chelsea. By general agreement, the address is identified as Wellington Square – and indeed Fleming biographer John Pearson went further by identifying the house as number 30 in

Wellington Square, Chelsea, Bond's home in the novels.

his 1973 work of fiction, *James Bond: The Authorised Biography of 007* – but other squares have been suggested, among them Markham Square almost opposite Wellington Square. Whatever the case, a walk along the King's Road and into the various discreet and exclusive residential areas off the thoroughfare takes you squarely into Bond's world.

Carlyle Mansions, Cheyne Walk, SW3 5LS

Ian and Ann Fleming lived at Carlyle Mansions in Chelsea for little more than a year. The flat they leased there from 1952 was tall ceilinged, opulent, and extravagantly decorated, but Ian was determined that it was no place to bring up his son Caspar, born the following year, and the Flemings moved out soon after.

119 Cheyne Walk, SW10 0ES

Ian Fleming's mother, Evelyn, acquired three properties along and behind Cheyne Walk in Chelsea in 1923 and connected them to create a single, spacious, home that served as a London base and a suitable venue for entertaining guests and hosting parties. One of them, number 119, was once the studio of painter J.M.W. Turner and naturally the place became known as Turner's House. (A plaque above

Carlyle Mansions, one of several of Ian Fleming's London residences.

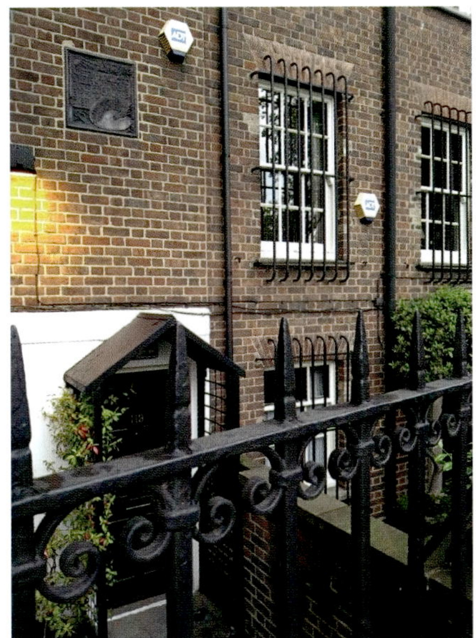

119 Cheyne Walk, formerly home to Evelyn Fleming and, before her, J.M.W. Turner.

the front door records the connection.) Fleming moved in with his mother and lived there until 1936.

LAMBETH

42 Roupell Street, SE1 8TB
For the sequence in NO TIME TO DIE when Bond (Daniel Craig) and Moneypenny (Naomie Harris) visit Q's (Ben Whishaw) home in London, a scene was shot outside 42 Roupell Street. The location doubled for the exterior of Q's house and Bond and Moneypenny were filmed knocking at the door. The scene was cut, but eagle-eyed viewers, sharing Q's viewpoint, can see the other side of the street behind Bond and Moneypenny in Q's video doorbell monitor. What is

Roupell Street, Q's home in NO TIME TO DIE.

shown is number 43 Roupell Street and commercial premises on the corner of Roupell Street and Cornwall Road.

C.P. Hart Bathrooms, Railway Arch, 213 Newnham Terrace, Hercules Road, SE1 7DR

An underpass next to the entrance of C.P. Hart Bathrooms provides the location in NO TIME TO DIE for Bond's garage, where he stores his Aston Martin V8 (last seen in THE LIVING DAYLIGHTS). Bond (Daniel Craig) lifts the garage door, pulls the covers away from the car, and speeds away. He turns right into the underpass, then immediately right again into another tunnel and into the streets of London. The underpass runs between the entrance of C.P. Hart on Newnham Terrace and Centaur Street. Bond's garage is at the C.P. Hart end of the underpass and next to the C.P. Hart's customer car park, which served as the tunnel into which 007 turned right again.

Westminster Bridge (east end), Westminster Bridge Road, SE1 7PB

Ever the model – before becoming James Bond in 1968, he advertised Fry's

Bond finds this Lambeth underpass an ideal place to garage his Aston Martin.

Chocolates – George Lazenby threw himself into the publicity for ON HER MAJESTY'S SECRET SERVICE prior to its release in 1969, resulting in some iconic imagery. In one photographic shoot, Lazenby posed gun in hand on the plinth of a lamppost on the south bank of the River Thames, with the Houses of Parliament forming a dramatic backdrop. The images at once encapsulated Lazenby's bravado, late 1960s' cool, and the notion of Bond as defender of the realm. The lamppost has since become a magnet for Bond lovers, who clamber up on to the plinth and adopt the famous Bond pose. To add to its renown, the lamppost made an appearance in a Bond film some forty-five years after Lazenby's publicity shoot. During the denouement of SPECTRE, Madeleine Swann (Léa Seydoux) passes the lamppost and ascends the steps to reach the bridge where Bond (Daniel Craig) is confronting Blofeld (Christoph Waltz). For many years, the lamppost had fallen into disrepair – that it appears to be working in SPECTRE may be due to some movie magic – but after a determined social media campaign by Bond fan Ian Jacklin, the lamppost was restored by Lambeth Council. To reach the lamppost, walk down the steps on the south side of the east end of Westminster Bridge. The lamppost is immediately on your right on a granite plinth that stands at the end of the stone handrail of the steps.

The 'James Bond' lamppost off Westminster Bridge, made famous by George Lazenby.

The lamppost is not the only point of interest for Bond lovers on or close to Westminster Bridge. Climb the steps again and cross the width of the bridge, watching out for traffic, cyclists and pedestrians, to reach the set of steps on the north side of the east end of the bridge (signposted The Queen's Walk). Go down the first six or seven steps to a mid-staircase level. You will have on your right the granite plinth that supports the South Bank Lion, a stone statue of a lion erected after

The South Bank Lion plinth with the secret door to Vauxhall Cross Station.

the Second World War at the request of King George VI. Take a few steps to the north face of the plinth. The door there doubled in DIE ANOTHER DAY as the secret entrance to Vauxhall Cross underground station, where Bond (Pierce Brosnan) meets M (Judi Dench) and finds Q (John Cleese) with Q-Branch relics of Bond adventures past.

The South Bank Lion and its plinth, as well as the bridge itself, are prominent in the final scene between Bond and Blofeld in SPECTRE. The helicopter that is carrying Blofeld crashes on to the bridge, and armed police officers quickly reach the scene and close the bridge off. Bond arrives and makes his way over to Blofeld, who has crawled out of the helicopter. Rather than kill Blofeld, Bond hands him over to M (Ralph Fiennes) and walks towards Swann, who is waiting at the east end of the bridge, the lion being in clear view. Bond throws his gun over the parapet of the bridge, a gesture that seemingly serves notice of his resignation from the service. It is possible that the gun remains at the bottom of the river today.

SIS Building, 85 Albert Embankment, SE1 7TP
www.sis.gov.uk

From GOLDENEYE to SPECTRE, the building that is the real-life headquarters of the British Secret Intelligence Service (SIS), popularly known as MI6, also served as the location of secret service headquarters in the fictional world of James Bond. The use of the SIS Building or Vauxhall Cross in GOLDENEYE coincided with a new openness for Britain's intelligence and security services; it was only in 1994 – GOLDENEYE was released in 1995 – that the British government officially acknowledged the existence of the SIS and that its chief was known by the letter C. It was in 1994 also that the building, designed by architect

The SIS Building, one of the best-known buildings in London, thanks to James Bond.

Terry Farrell, was opened, construction work having commenced in 1988. In *SPECTRE*, we witness the razing of a bomb-damaged Vauxhall Cross in a controlled demolition hastened by Blofeld. Fortunately for the real spies and analysts, the building still exists, but naturally it is closed to the public. Excellent views of the building, however, can be had from Vauxhall Bridge and from any number of tourist boats that ply their trade up and down the River Thames.

4 Albert Square, Stockwell, SW8 1BU

Roger Moore, who was born in 1927, lived as a child in Albert Square in Stockwell. He recalled in his 2008 memoir, *My Word is My Bond*, that he and his parents occupied a third-floor flat at, he thought, number four. The house is one property within a block of five terrace houses, each three-and-a-half storeys high. The terrace has been listed by Historic England for its architectural significance, but, alas, there is no blue plaque to record its association with the actor who was the James Bond of a generation, having starred in seven Bond films between 1973 and 1985.

RICHMOND-ON-THAMES

Royal Botanic Gardens, Kew, Richmond, TW9 3AE

www.kew.org

As Bond (Daniel Craig) says in SKYFALL, everyone needs a hobby. Even Bond's chief, M, has one. In *On Her Majesty's Secret Service*, we learn that he is a devotee of orchids, and that he occasionally reads Nero Wolfe stories by mystery writer Rex Stout. (In the film of the book, orchidology is replaced by lepidoptery, or the study of butterflies.) M has a contact at Kew in Richmond – an assistant to Summerhayes, the botanic garden's orchid specialist – who supplies M with specimens, one of which, an autumn lady's tresses (*Spiranthes spiralis*), M is pleased to show Bond when 007 visits his home, Quarterdeck. The Royal Botanic Gardens hold some 2,500 types of orchid in its collection, and many of these can be seen by the public in the Tropical Nursery, the Princess of Wales Conservatory, the Palm House, the Rock Garden, and the wildflower areas.

SOUTHWARK

City Hall, 110 The Queen's Walk, SE1 2AA
The former home of the Greater London Authority (GLA) on The Queen's Walk doubled as the headquarters of the Joint Intelligence Service, headed by Max Denbigh or 'C' (Andrew Scott), in SPECTRE. The domed, helmet-shaped, glass-fronted building was designed by Norman Foster and completed in 2002. A notable feature of the design is the helical staircase, which runs around the ten storeys of the building and appears in scenes in which M (Ralph Fiennes) and C discuss the future of Britain's intelligence services but are not quite seeing eye to eye. The GLA moved out

City Hall, used as the headquarters of the Joint Intelligence Service in SPECTRE.

of the building in 2021, and at present it remains empty and closed to visitors.

Imperial War Museum, Lambeth Road, SE1 6HZ
www.iwm.org.uk

The Secret War is a permanent exhibition at the Imperial War Museum that displays some of the gadgets, weapons and other tricks of the trade of covert operations and tells the stories of Second World War agents, special forces, and Cold War spies. And in an exhibition of real-life agents, James Bond is never far away. Visitors entering the exhibition are met by a display that includes a poster of CASINO ROYALE, accompanied by the words, 'It's easy to mistake spy fiction for reality'. Turning the corner takes visitors to a short film, in which the real begins to be separated from the fictional; the video is soundtracked by music from the Bond films, and various images from the films appear on screen.

The exhibition displays gadgets – many designed for use in the Second World War – that are echoed in the Bond films and to a much lesser extent in the books. Ordinary items such as fountain pens, clothes brushes, razors, shoes and so on were used to conceal maps, secret messages, compasses, invisible ink, wire, tools and much more, and can be seen in the display cases. There is information too on

Second World War agents who became famous for their remarkable wartime stories, among them Wing Commander Yeo-Thomas and Fitzroy Maclean, both of whom have been claimed as inspirations for Bond.

TOWER HAMLETS

Canary Wharf Underground Station, Heron Quays Road, E14 4HJ

Ken Adam was responsible for some of the most iconic sets seen in the Bond films, and naturally his work has influenced others, both within and outside the film industry. As Adam revealed in 2008 in conversation with Christopher Frayling to coincide with the publication of *Ken Adam Designs the Movies: James Bond and Beyond*, one person who has looked to the set designer's work is renowned architect Norman Foster, who took inspiration for his design of Canary Wharf Underground Station from the sets for THE SPY WHO LOVED ME. Looking at the underground station, the source of the inspiration seems clear. The main hall of the station contains elements that resemble the docking bay of the Liparus, Stromberg's submarine-swallowing supertanker. The central columns, the domed roof, and the black side panels of the station all find some equivalence in the design of the tanker. And it is possible that Foster turned to another classic Adam set. When you next visit Canary Wharf station, exit via the escalators and look up at the glass and metal roof overhead. If you think you have seen that roof somewhere before, then you are probably thinking of the grille in Dr No's ante-room in DR NO. There is certainly a similarity.

Glengall Bridge, Pepper Street, Millwall, Isle of Dogs, E14 9RD

Before NO TIME TO DIE broke the record, THE WORLD IS NOT ENOUGH had the distinction of having the longest pre-titles sequence in a Bond film. Much of the sequence's fifteen or so minutes is taken up by an epic boat chase along the Thames in the heart of London. Having witnessed the assassination of Sir Robert King (David Calder) at MI6 headquarters, Bond (Pierce Brosnan) borrows Q's (Desmond Llewelyn) 'fishing boat' – a sleek, jet-powered stealth boat with all the usual refinements – and is propelled out of the SIS Building and on to the river in pursuit of the assassin (Maria Grazia Cucinotta), known as the Cigar Girl. Bond gives chase, following the Cigar Girl's equally powerful boat downstream and utterly ignoring the iconic landmarks of London – the Houses of Parliament, Westminster Bridge, Waterloo Bridge and Tower Bridge, among others – that whizz by as he heads towards the Docklands.

Several landmarks are well worth visiting at a more leisurely pace. Glengall Bridge, a bascule-type

Glengall Bridge in London's Docklands stopped the Cigar Girl in her tracks in THE WORLD IS NOT ENOUGH.

construction that is raised and lowered like a drawbridge, is prominent in one scene. In the film, the bridge comes down, blocking the Cigar Girl's route and forcing her to change course. Fortunately, one does not need a boat to visit the bridge, which separates the Millwall Inner Dock and Outer Dock. Take the Docklands Light Railway and alight at Crossharbour DLR station. Walk a short distance along Westward Parade, which becomes Pepper Street, until you reach the bridge.

Ornamental Canal, Wapping Lane, St George in the East, Wapping, E1W 3HZ

The Ornamental Canal was the scene of two exciting moments in the epic boat chase that takes up much of the pre-titles sequence in THE WORLD IS NOT ENOUGH. At one point, Bond (Pierce Brosnan) powers his 'Q Boat' along a stretch of water towards a boathouse. He crashes through it and ends up on a busy street, obliging him – still somehow keeping the boat in motion – to negotiate road junctions, cars, and

The Ornamental Canal at Tobacco Dock was a key location in the boat chase in THE WORLD IS NOT ENOUGH.

a London bus. The stretch of water runs along the south side of Tobacco Dock and the shot on screen of Bond approaching the boathouse is best viewed from Wapping Lane at the point that the lane crosses the canal.

If you descend on to the lower pathway on the north side of the Ornamental Canal and continue to walk west – passing two seemingly life-size model ships, the *Sea Lark* and the *Three Sisters*, which should be on your right – you will reach a bend in the canal. It is at this bend where Bond, making the sharp turn at speed before his approach to the boathouse, soaks two parking enforcement officers (who were genuine traffic wardens and were already known to British audiences, having featured in a BBC reality TV series called *The Clampers*), rather unfairly giving audiences a collective feeling of *schadenfreude*.

The best means of getting to the Ornamental Canal is to take the Docklands Light Railway (DLR) and alight at Shadwell. It is a ten-minute walk, via Cable Street, St George Gardens and

The bend in the Ornamental Canal where two parking enforcement officers were splashed by Bond in THE WORLD IS NOT ENOUGH.

Wapping Lane, from the station to the canal. Tobacco Dock is well signposted.

Trinity Buoy Wharf, 64 Orchard Place, Poplar, E14 0JW
www.trinitybuoywharf.com

While somehow managing to traverse dry land in his 'Q Boat' in his pursuit of the assassin known as the Cigar Girl during the pre-titles sequence of THE WORLD IS NOT ENOUGH, Bond (Pierce Brosnan) takes a shortcut through a busy restaurant, leaving diners both shaken and stirred, but allowing him to regain the Thames in front of the O2 arena or Millennium Dome. The restaurant scene was filmed at the Chain Store, a building that was constructed in the late nineteenth century to store mooring chains and buoys, but today, as part of the Trinity Buoy Wharf arts and creative centre, serves as an events venue. The centre is open to the public; alight at Canning Town tube station or East India DLR station.

SOUTH AND SOUTH-EAST

BERKSHIRE

Hotel de Paris (site of), 1 Braybank, Old Mill Lane, Bray, SL6 2BQ

In *The Spy Who Loved Me*, Vivienne Michel's boyfriend, Derek Mallaby, takes her to the smart Hotel de Paris on the banks of the Thames at Bray. Like many places mentioned in the Bond novels, the hotel was real enough. Established in 1928, the hotel was named after the Café de Paris in London, which was also owned by the hotel's proprietors. In Ian Fleming's day it boasted a terrace bar, a lawn bar, a ballroom, a lounge, riverside gardens and an outside dance area, as well as a restaurant and accommodation. According to a brochure dating to the 1950s, the best rooms, comprising a double bedroom with adjoining sitting room and private bathroom, were available at £5 and 5 shillings per night (approximately £110 in today's money). Vivienne and Derek stayed for a lunch of smoked salmon, roast chicken and ice cream. This would have cost at least 14 shillings and 6 pence per person, or about £15 today. The hotel had little time to benefit from any publicity its association with James Bond might have brought. Two years after *The Spy Who Loved Me* was published, the hotel was closed to be redeveloped into flats and houses, and today the site is known as the Braybank Estate.

The Brocas, SL4 6BW, and Cuckoo Weir, SL4 5JH, Eton

Thinking back while alone in the Dreamy Pines Motor Hotel in the Adirondacks in *The Spy Who Loved Me* to her love affair with bounder Derek Mallaby, Vivienne Michel recalls their trips along the Thames in an electric canoe, languidly chugging downriver towards Windsor, past the riparian landmarks of Queen's Eyot, Boveney Lock, Coocoo Weir (sic), and Brocas meadows.

These points of reference can still be found on the map today, being situated along a 5km stretch of the Thames between Dorney and Eton. Probably the best means of seeing them is, like Vivienne Michell, to take a boat, and there are several boat companies in

The Brocas at Eton, a regular haunt for Vivienne Michel in **The Spy Who Loved Me**, *as well as Ian Fleming.*

Windsor that offer tours along the river and take in all the relevant locations. Some tour companies operate a return route from Windsor to Maidenhead, allowing Bond lovers to reach another location from the novel, Bray.

Alternatively, the locations can be visited on foot or bicycle via the Thames Path that extends along the north bank of the river. Start the walk (or cycle) at the Brocas, riverside meadows that can be reached via a path off Brocas Street in Eton close to the Eton side of Windsor Bridge, and continue west. Coocoo Weir (actually Cuckoo Weir; had Ian Fleming never seen the place name written down?), which is the next landmark to be reached, is not signposted, but at the mouth of the weir there is a wooden bridge (Long Bridge, National Grid Reference SU955777) into which a series of charmingly poetic lines have been inscribed. Given that Cuckoo Weir at this point is lined with dense vegetation and the water is not wholly

Cuckoo Weir, where Vivienne Michel would swim.

Boveney Lock, through which Vivienne Michel passes in The Spy Who Loved Me.

inviting, Vivienne Michel's reference to her swimming there might seem puzzling to today's readers. At the time Fleming was writing, however, the weir, complete with stone- and wood-revetted banks and steps for access, had long been used by Eton boys for swimming, including, no doubt, Fleming himself. Contemporaneous mapping marks this as the site of the 'Humane Swimming Baths', suggesting that this swimming area was open to the public. Traces of the revetments still exist in the part of the weir just past the bend immediately beyond its mouth.

Continuing the walk further west, one will reach Boveney Lock (SL4 6QQ), and beyond that (and past Dorney Rowing Lake), Queen's Eyot, an island in the Thames.

Eton College, Windsor, SL4 6DW
www.etoncollege.com

Ian Fleming attended Eton College from 1921 to 1926. While he did not distinguish himself academically, he excelled in athletics and other individual sports, gaining the title of *Victor Ludorum* – Champion of the Games – in successive years (1925 and 1926). His experiences at the school left its mark on Fleming. We get clues of his time there from *The Spy Who Loved Me* – boating on the Thames, swimming in Cuckoo Weir, romantic interludes at Windsor's Regal Cinema – and he sent both his son Caspar and his literary creation James Bond to the school. As we learn in *You Only Live Twice*, however, Bond's time there was not successful; he left after only two halves following some trouble with a maid. Bond's days at Eton are cleverly reconstructed in Charlie Higson's *Young Bond* series, commencing with *SilverFin*.

Founded by King Henry VI in 1440, Eton College was known originally as Kynge's College of Our Ladye of Eton besyde Windesore, having been established to provide education to seventy poor boys who would then go on to King's College, Cambridge. At the centre of the college is School Yard, around which are grouped the College Chapel, which forms the southern range, the buildings of the Lower and Upper Schools, which form the western and northern ranges, and the cloister, which forms the eastern range. The college hall and kitchen are arranged around a smaller courtyard that adjoins School Yard. Public access to the school is naturally restricted, but guided tours of the principal buildings are conducted by the school from May to September. The Museum of Eton Life, which tells the story of the school from its inception to the present day, is open on Sundays and is accessed via Baldwin's Shore. Visitors continuing north along Slough Road, passing the chapel and School Yard on their right and Common Lane on their left, will

Looking through the porter's lodge of Eton College into School Yard.

reach the boys' house of Timbralls, also on their left, where the young Fleming resided.

Regal Cinema (site of), 113 Peascod Street, Windsor, SL4 1DN

Vivienne Michel and her lover Derek Mallaby end a romantic day in *The Spy Who Loved Me* at the Royalty Kinema in Farquhar Street. Several weeks later they return to the cinema, where, having secured a box (costing 12 shillings or £13 today) and a little privacy, they are caught *in flagrante delecto* by the cinema manager and are unceremoniously escorted out. Ian Fleming admitted to his friend Robert Harling that the episode closely mirrored a schoolboy experience of his own, claiming that it was a case of fiction copying fact. Perhaps to save embarrassment of the parties concerned, both the Royalty Kinema and Farquhar Street were products of Fleming's imagination. However, the Regal Cinema, originally the Windsor Kinema, did exist, and it is possible that Fleming had this in mind. The 700-odd seat cinema was located at 113 Peascod Street and closed in 1969. Following a

The site of the Regal Cinema, Windsor, which inspired Ian Fleming's Royalty Kinema.

period as a bingo hall, the space was converted for retail use and today is occupied by Superdry.

Windsor and Eton Central Station, Thames Street, Windsor, SL4 1PJ
When Derek Mallaby invites Vivienne Michel for a ride in his new car, Vivienne meets him at Windsor station, having taken the train at Paddington. This is Windsor and Eton Central station, not to be confused with Windsor and Eton Riverside station that connects the town with London Waterloo.

Hurley Lock, Mill Lane, Maidenhead, SL6 5ND
Hurley Lock on the River Thames by the village of Hurley is a very pleasant spot for picnics, walking the dog, and generally relaxing by the water's edge. Bond (Sean Connery) thinks so too and stops here in FROM RUSSIA WITH LOVE for champagne and lovemaking with his companion Sylvia Trench (Eunice Gayson) before being called back to the office. Pinpointing the exact location of the scene, in which we see James and Sylvia reclining in a punt,

The ornate entrance to Windsor and Eton Central Station.

James getting out and walking to his car – a 1935 Bentley 3½-litre Drophead Coupé – and Sylvia following, is not easy. That they are on the south bank is evident from the flow of the river from west to east, but the natural and built environment around the lock has changed since the scene was filmed, and identification is not helped by the tight camera angles and editing room magic, not to mention the various river channels that are present here. A likely location, however, is on the east side of the lock on the south bank just off the Thames Path, where there is, beyond a row of trees, a meadow or field, as seen in the background when James is at the car. There is also a lane (Mill Lane) and trackway that would allow the film-makers to get the car to the river's edge.

Whatever the precise location of the scene, Hurley Lock makes an idyllic day out for Bond lovers. To reach the lock, turn off the A4130 Henley Road towards Hurley village and continue through the village, past a couple of public houses on your right and a village shop on your

Hurley Lock, where Bond and Sylvia Trench picnic in FROM RUSSIA WITH LOVE.

left, until you reach a car park on the left. Park here, then follow the signs to the lock and walk along the footpath to the river. At the river, cross over the footbridge and continue walking along the Thames Path – now on one of the islands within the river – past the lock. Cross over another footbridge to get back to the south bank and the approximate location of the scene.

BUCKINGHAMSHIRE

Stowe Gardens, Buckingham, MK18 5EQ
www.nationaltrust.org.uk;
www.landmarktrust.org.uk

The landscape gardens at Stowe became the Scottish estate of Sir Robert King (David Calder) in THE WORLD IS NOT ENOUGH. Following his premature death at MI6 headquarters in London, the funeral of Sir Robert, with, among others, Bond (Pierce Brosnan), M (Judi Dench), and Sir Robert's daughter Elektra King (Sophie Marceau) in attendance, takes place at a chapel on his estate. A lone piper sounds a mournful note from the tower, and the mourners leave the chapel and walk along a tree-lined path to their vehicles.

In reality, the chapel is the Gothic Temple, which was designed by James Gibbs under the direction of Viscount Cobham, owner of Stowe, in 1741. The temple, prominent on top of a hill, formed part of a walk entitled 'the Path

The Gothic Temple in Stowe Park, seen in THE WORLD IS NOT ENOUGH.

of Liberty', the viscount dedicating the building to the 'liberties of our ancestors'. The temple is set in sight of Stowe School within a landscape that is today managed by the National Trust. To reach the temple, after parking in the site's main car park, walk along Bellgate Drive, which ends at a lake. Take one of the paths to the right (keeping the school to your left) and follow the path round until you reach the temple, crossing the Palladian Bridge on the way. Access to the building itself is restricted – it is leased by the Landmark Trust and available for hire as a holiday property – but, if not staying in the building, visitors can still explore its external features and walk along the tree-lined path. Incidentally, Stowe offers another Bond connection: David Niven, who starred as Sir James Bond in the 1967 film adaptation of *Casino Royale*, attended the school as a child.

Finmere Airfield, near Finmere Aerodrome Farm, Barton Hartshorn, Buckingham, MK18 4JA

Never trust a SPECTRE agent. In YOU ONLY LIVE TWICE, having been captured by Mr Osato's men in Kobe in Japan while investigating the cargo ship, the *Ning-Po*, Bond (Sean Connery) is at the mercy of SPECTRE's femme fatale, Helga Brandt (Karin Dor). Instead of interrogating Bond, however, Brandt releases him, and they escape in Brandt's small plane, a Meyers 200A.

It is, alas, a trick. Brandt secures Bond to his seat and parachutes out of the plane. The plane descends rapidly, but Bond manages to gain enough control of it to crash-land on an airstrip. He leaps out just before the plane explodes.

The crash-landing was filmed at Finmere airfield, near Buckingham, a former RAF base constructed in 1941, whose main role during the Second World War was to train bomber aircrews. After the war, the base returned to farmland (Finmere Aerodrome Farm is adjacent to the airstrip), but part of the site was retained and continues to serve as an airfield for civil aircraft. The site is best reached by car. Head west on the A421 from Buckingham and, as the road bypasses the southern end of the village of Tingewick, turn south into an unnamed lane that leads to Barton Hartshorn. Immediately after turning into the lane, pull over to the site and park up. The airfield is located very close to the junction with the main road and lies to the west of the lane. Access to the airstrip is not permitted at this location – it is fenced off and there is a sign reminding visitors that the site is an active airfield and to keep out – but there is a public footpath, Bernwood Jubilee Way, that runs between the airstrip and the A421. Walk along the footpath for about 400m. The path connects to another public footpath that

Finmere airfield stood in for a Japanese runway in YOU ONLY LIVE TWICE.

takes you across the concrete runway. But do watch out for low-flying aircraft!

Waddesdon Manor, Waddesdon, Aylesbury, HP18 0JH
waddesdon.org.uk

Waddesdon Manor, a grand, Renaissance-style house built for Baron Ferdinand de Rothschild in the late nineteenth century, could have been transplanted from the Loire Valley, and understandably the manor house has long attracted film crews after a picturesque slice of historic France within easy reach of Pinewood Studios. For the 1983 film NEVER SAY NEVER AGAIN – one of two Bond films to be released that year – the suite of rooms on the ground floor were transformed into a casino ostensibly in Nice on the French Riviera. Transformed is perhaps the wrong word, as, seeing those rooms even today, there appears to have been very little set dressing, with much of the original décor and furnishings being allowed to remain *in situ*. The most notable scene in the casino sequence is undoubtedly the high-stakes contest between Bond (Sean Connery) and Maximillian Largo (Klaus Maria Brandauer) at the computer game of 'Domination'. The game was set up in the dining room, and, apart from the replacement of the dining table with the computer game,

Waddesdon Manor, which was transformed into a casino in NEVER SAY NEVER AGAIN.

what is seen on screen – the mirror frames, the tapestries, curtains and marble panelling, naturally all French or of French design – can still be seen by visitors to the room today. At one point, Domino Petachi (Kim Basinger) stands by a doorway with a red room behind her. This is the red drawing room, which adjoins the dining room, and again many of the fittings seen in the film are original features that are still there today. The red carpeted staircase that Largo ascends – to his credit, very nonchalantly, given his defeat by Bond – is a staircase off the east gallery. His exit is viewed by audiences and casino-goers from the anteroom between the dining room and the conservatory.

Waddesdon Manor is a National Trust property set in a stunning landscape. Apart from the house itself, the grounds (complete with aviary) are well worth a visit, and there is a shop selling the Rothschild family's own wine (it owns several vineyards in France). At Christmas, the house usually puts on a magical light show, and inside, the rooms are bedecked with seasonal decorations.

The Royal Saracens Head, 6–8 London End, Beaconsfield, HP9 2JH
www.theroyalsaracens.co.uk

This eighteenth-century coaching inn makes a fleeting appearance in THUNDERBALL. We see a black car drive through the arch of the public house into a courtyard. From a telephone box on the corner of the road, SPECTRE agent Count Lippe (Guy Doleman) phones Fiona Volpe (Luciana Paluzzi), who at that point is keeping Major Duval (Paul Stassino) entertained in his room at the inn, to alert her that Angelo Palazzi (who has taken on the appearance of Major Duval and is naturally also played by Paul Stassino) has arrived. Following SPECTRE's elaborate scheme, Palazzi knocks at Duval's door and murders Duval with poison delivered by means of a spray. He then leaves for the airbase to take Duval's place on a Vulcan bomber, allowing him to hijack it and its payload of two nuclear bombs.

The inn, now an elegant gastropub, is located on the corner of London End (A40) and Windsor End and is just minutes from junction 2 of the M40. The view of the road and the exterior of the inn is largely unchanged since the scene was filmed, but the arch into the courtyard has since been closed off to vehicles and converted into the main entrance to the pub. The telephone box has been removed, although there is another one within sight of the pub a few metres down Windsor End. There are plenty of parking spaces along London End and Windsor End, but finding an unoccupied space can be difficult. Be prepared to cruise up and down the road until a space becomes available.

The Royal Saracens Head provided accommodation for SPECTRE agents in THUNDERBALL.

Church of St Giles, Stoke Green, Slough, SL2 4PG

In FOR YOUR EYES ONLY, the film-makers made a rare reference to events in Bond's past when they had 007 (Roger Moore) visit the grave of his wife, Tracy Bond, whom he had married in ON HER MAJESTY'S SECRET SERVICE, but who was murdered by Irma Bunt shortly after the wedding. While at the graveside, Bond is alerted by the vicar (Fred Bryant) that he is wanted at the office; some sort of emergency, he says. An MI6 helicopter – bearing the name of its cover organisation, Universal Exports – lands in a field next to the church and flies Bond away, the vicar ominously making the sign of the cross at the churchyard lychgate as it does so.

The scene was filmed in the churchyard of St Giles' Church in the hamlet of Stoke Green near Stoke Poges. The headstone of Tracy Bond's grave was, of course, a prop and removed after filming, but its approximate position, next to the

The graveyard of St Giles's Church, Stoke Green.

Gray's Field next to St Giles's Church, Stoke Green.

stone-bordered grave of Alice Isbell and a plaque on the ground that marks the grave of Diana Mary Lacey, can be found in the extension of the graveyard beyond the churchyard wall, a few steps away from the path.

The helicopter landed in Gray's Field – named after the poet Thomas Gray (1716–71), who is buried in the church – adjacent to the churchyard. The field is accessible to the public, having been presented to the National Trust in 1924 when it was purchased to preserve the rural setting of the church.

There is ample parking if visiting the church by car. Turning into the lane that leads to the church from Church Lane, you will find a small parking area on the right-hand side. If full, there is a larger parking area on the south side of Church Lane opposite the lane for the church.

Stoke Park, Park Road, Stoke Poges, SL2 4PG

www.stokepark.com

The golf club that is perhaps most closely associated with James Bond is Stoke Park in Buckinghamshire, which doubled for Royal St Marks in GOLDFINGER. That the golf scenes should appear so convincing, and in time become so celebrated, is thanks in no small measure to Sean Connery's burgeoning fondness for the game. Connery had been introduced to golf during the filming of FROM RUSSIA WITH LOVE, and in anticipation of the filming of the sequence in GOLDFINGER had begun to take lessons. Additionally, golf professionals worked on Connery's swing to give him the appearance of a player with a handicap appropriate for Bond. EON Productions returned to Stoke Park to film a scene for TOMORROW NEVER DIES. The ballroom there doubled for Bond's Hamburg hotel room.

For many years, Stoke Park celebrated its links to Bond, hosting 007-related events and displaying memorabilia, photographs and objects from the films in the 'James Bond Hall of Fame'. The club, for many years closed, has reopened after renovation and change of ownership.

Chalfont Park House, Chalfont St Peter, Gerrards Cross, SL9 0QA

Shrublands, the fictional health clinic that Bond visits, not without some reluctance, in *Thunderball*, is represented on screen – at least in the exterior shots – in the film of the same name by Chalfont Park House, a mansion with mid-eighteenth-century origins, but remodelled in the nineteenth century in the Gothic style, complete with battlemented turrets, bays and parapets. The building is not normally open to the public, but it is possible to drive up to the house and take in the impressive front of the building. The house is approached via

Chalfont Park House doubled for Shrublands health farm in THUNDERBALL.

a lane, Chalfont Park, that runs parallel with the A413, the main road from which Chalfont Lane is reached. The house is midway along the lane, past the Gerrards Park Golf Course and the Buttercups Nursery.

Thames Lawn, St Peter Street, Marlow, SL7 1QA

When Bond (George Lazenby) visits M's home in ON HER MAJESTY'S SECRET SERVICE, where he hopes to convince M (Bernard Lee) to put him back on to Operation Bedlam now that he has a lead on the whereabouts of Ernst Stavro Blofeld (Telly Savalas), we see him in his Aston Martin DB5, driving along a chocolate box street of historic, eighteenth-century buildings and through a gateway into the drive of a large house. The street is St Peter Street in Marlow and Bond is driving south towards the public slipway on the River Thames. On screen, there is little to see on Bond's side of the car, but on the passenger's side, we catch a glimpse of a sign of a public house. This is the Two Brewers, which remains open for business today, complete with an identical pub sign. The site of M's house is on the south side of the public house. In the film, the house was called Quarterdeck but in reality it is Thames Lawn. The house that represented M's home has since been replaced by another, but the street-fronted brick and flint wall and gateway into the drive are as they were on screen.

St Peter Street can, of course, be reached by car, but given that Marlow is a very popular, picturesque town on the Thames, the roads are often rammed with traffic and parking is difficult, especially in summer. Do come into town as early in the day as possible and park in one of the public car parks near the town centre or in a side street on the outskirts of the town. It may then mean a trek to St Peter Street, but at least you will work up a thirst, justifying a visit to the Two Brewers for suitable refreshment. The best way to get to St Peter Street is to walk down High Street towards the Thames. At All

Thames Lawn and the Two Brewers public house, Marlow.

Saints' Church, turn into the churchyard and then into an alleyway on the northern side of the church grounds. St Peter Street is at the end of the alleyway, and you will come out at the precise spot seen in the film.

KENT

Kent Police Headquarters, Sutton Road, Maidstone, ME15 9BJ

Bond's rehabilitation following his brainwashing at the hands of Colonel Boris of the KGB and attempted assassination of M at the start of *The Man with the Golden Gun* is intense: six weeks of electric-convulsive treatment and analysis at a discreet convalescent home in Kent known as The Park, and hours of gun practice at the shooting range at Kent Police headquarters in Maidstone. Fuelled by his hatred of the Soviet system that almost destroyed him, Bond gets through it, and he is pronounced fit for duty by M and handed his mission. Bond's destination: Jamaica. His target: Francisco Scaramanga.

M, or more likely Moneypenny, would have needed to book Bond's sessions at the shooting range as far in advance as possible, because it was a busy place, being used not only by police officers, but also by shooting clubs and associations from across the county. For example, the range had hosted, not long before Bond's visits, the final of the Kent County Small Rifle Association's short-range championship, and a small-bore shooting competition for cadet units.

At the time that Ian Fleming was writing *The Man with the Golden Gun*, the headquarters of the Kent Police was on Sutton Road to the south-east of

Kent Police Headquarters, where James Bond practises his marksmanship.

Maidstone town centre, and it remains there today. Access to the complex is understandably restricted; visitors may, of course, step into the public entrance of the building, but the site of the shooting range will be out of bounds. The buildings themselves can be seen from Sutton Road (A474) and can be reached easily by car – follow signs for Sutton Valence and Headcorn – or by bus (take the number 12 to Tenterden from outside the Royal Star Arcade – another literary Bond location – and alight at the Shepway Sutton Road Police HQ stop).

Junction of King Street and Gabriel's Hill, Maidstone, ME14 1DE

When in *Moonraker* Sir Hugo Drax reaches the congested streets of Maidstone en route to London from his rocket base near Dover, his passenger up front – Special Branch agent Gala Brand, posing as Drax's secretary – sees an opportunity to nab Drax's notebook, filled with critical information about the rocket launch, from his hip pocket. Drax's Mercedes 300 S, making its way slowly westwards along King Street, is halted at the traffic lights at the junction with Gabriel's Hill. The lights turn green and Drax manoeuvres the car smartly around the family saloon in front that was frustrating him so much. As Brand is thrown towards Drax, she removes the notebook, hiding it within the folds of her coat.

Brand would not have the same opportunity were Drax to make the journey today. Apart from the fact that he would bypass Maidstone altogether and take the M20 motorway, King Street at the junction with Gabriel's Hill is partially pedestrianised, with traffic through King Street and into the High Street being restricted to buses and taxis. What is more, the traffic lights have long gone, and the necessity to wear seatbelts means that Brand could not have been thrown towards Drax.

The junction of King Street and Gabriel's Hill, Maidstone. Sir Hugo Drax's Mercedes would have stopped where the taxi is parked.

The Royal Star Arcade, 15–17 High Street, Maidstone, ME14 1JL
As Sir Hugo Drax races away from the traffic lights at the junction of King Street and Gabriel's Hill in his Mercedes 300 S, it is not the end of his frustrations. Continuing into the High Street, Drax sees two women and a boy using a zebra crossing by the Royal Star hotel and, with no intention of stopping, calculates his chances of getting through the crossing without hitting the pedestrians.

The Royal Star hotel was established in the sixteenth century as a coaching inn, but the brick-built, three-storey building that stands today dates to the eighteenth century. The hotel became a popular venue for civic functions – society dinner dances, public auctions, lectures and talks, exhibitions, and a meeting place for societies and trade organisations – and boasted some appropriately large spaces, including the King's Hall and Queen's Banqueting Hall. The Cavalier's Bar featured historic panels that told the story of the hotel's connection with the events of the English Civil War (1642–51). At the time

***The Royal Star, the hotel, now a shopping centre, mentioned in* Moonraker.**

Drax was racing past the Royal Star (*Moonraker* was published in 1955), the hotel had not long before hosted a dance for Maidstone farmers, with music provided by Stanley Norman and his orchestra, and in 1957 it would accommodate a meeting of cricket's top brass in Kent that, as the *Kent Messenger* newspaper claimed, would have far-reaching consequences for the sport in the county. The hotel was sympathetically converted into a boutique shopping centre in 1989 – many period features were retained – and remains open to shoppers to this day. The zebra crossing has been removed, but there is a pedestrian crossing a hundred metres or so further along the High Street.

Sir Thomas Wyatt Beefeater, London Road, Maidstone, ME16 0HG
www.beefeater.co.uk

Having in *Moonraker* purloined Sir Hugo Drax's notebook that contain important calculations relating to the launch of the Moonraker rocket, Special Branch agent Gala Brand is desperate to find a place where she can compare Drax's figures with her own. She persuades Drax to pull up to the front of the Sir Thomas Wyatt inn on London Road on the way out of Maidstone. Brand races into the inn and into the ladies' toilets, where she flicks through the notebook and is horrified to discover that Drax intends to direct the atomic missile, not harmlessly into the North Sea, but into the heart of London.

The Sir Thomas Wyatt inn would have been a familiar sight to Ian Fleming, who would have passed it, and perhaps occasionally stopped there, on his many journeys through Kent to or from his way from St Margaret's Bay, where he had a home, or the Royal St George's golf club, of which he was a regular member. Before the construction of the M20 motorway, London Road at Allington would have been the main route for motorists on their way towards London after Maidstone or approaching the town from London. Its prominent position made the inn a local landmark. In 1948, ahead of the Olympic Games that summer in London, a stage of the journey of the Olympic torch, which had been carried from Dover (having been lit at Olympia in Greece), ended at the Sir Thomas Wyatt, where a crowd of spectators and the county's great and the good had gathered.

The inn continues to thrive today in the form of a Beefeater restaurant. It no longer serves as a hotel, but Bond lovers visiting the location may like to stay in a Premier Inn hotel that adjoins the restaurant. The Sir Thomas Wyatt is often busy, especially at weekends, so booking a table for an evening meal is recommended. For anyone staying at the Premier Inn, breakfast is served in the Sir Thomas Wyatt.

The Sir Thomas Wyatt inn, where Gala Brand pretends to take a comfort break.

Duck Inn, Pett Bottom, Canterbury, CT4 5PB
www.duckpettbottom.co.uk

We learn in Ian Fleming's penultimate novel, *You Only Live Twice*, that after his parents died, the young James was taken in by his aunt Charmian Bond, who lived in a cottage near the Duck Inn in Pett Bottom, a village near Canterbury. We cannot be sure whether Fleming had a real cottage in mind for Aunt Charmian, but there is a cottage and a farmhouse on School Lane just round the corner from the Duck Inn that might fit the bill. A blue plaque on the building records Ian Fleming's connection with the public house, which also celebrates the association inside.

Old Palace, Old Palace Road, Bekesbourne, Canterbury, CT4 5ES
During her relationship with Ian, Ann Fleming long had hopes of moving to a grand country house. She had her heart set on Wiltshire or Gloucestershire, but Ian wanted to stay close to the Royal St George's golf club at Sandwich. In the

end, Ann and Ian decided on the Old Palace in the village of Bekesbourne, south of Canterbury, and moved there in 1957.

The Old Palace, comprising a two-storey mansion, several other buildings, and extensive grounds, was suitably grand. It also had history. The site was first settled during the Roman period, and in the late fourteenth or early fifteenth century, a manor house and associated buildings were erected. In 1540, the land was acquired by Thomas Cranmer, Archbishop of Canterbury, who built a palace on the site. The palace was considerably enlarged in the later sixteenth century by Archbishop Matthew Parker, and further modifications were made by Archbishop Whitgift in the last decade of the sixteenth century. The palace did not survive for much longer, however. In the mid-seventeenth century, during the English Civil War, the house was largely pulled down and the materials sold off. Just the gatehouse and traces of the stables and housekeeper's house survived, which were subsequently incorporated into a new house built in the eighteenth century. This was the Old Palace, which the Flemings would later occupy.

With its tall chimneys and crenellated parapet surrounding the attic, the main house has pretensions of something grander, though its striking white facade contrasts with the red brick of the genuine Tudor gatehouse, which still

The Old Palace, Bekesbourne, home briefly to Ian and Ann Fleming.

bears the initials, inscribed in stone, of Thomas Cranmer. Despite its colourful history, or perhaps because of it, Ann was miserable in the house. She complained about ghostly sounds and bangs inside and the noise of passing trains outside.

The house is not open to the public, but visitors to St Peter's Church are able to catch a sight of the house as they walk along Old Palace Road, which is about 500m south-east of Bekesbourne railway station.

Portrait Bench, Marine Parade, Dover, CT16 1LA

Ian Fleming's strong connection with the district of Dover is commemorated by a near-life-size silhouetted representation in metal of the author on the town's Marine Parade. Fleming is one of three figures that form the Portrait Bench on the Dover seafront, the others being wartime singer Dame Vera Lynn and 2012 Olympic torchbearer Jamie Clarke. Parking is available along the seafront, or instead one may park in town and walk to the bench via an underpass beneath the busy A20.

Royal Café (site of), 5 Bench Street, Dover, CT16 1JH

Moonraker sees James Bond, having awoken at seven o'clock at Drax's rocket establishment near Deal and eager for a good breakfast, drive into Dover and head to the Café Royal, a

The Portrait Bench in Dover that gives Ian Fleming a permanent view of the sea.

Atina House, the site of the Royal Café, the inspiration for Ian Fleming's Café Royal.

modest restaurant run by an Italian–Swiss family, where he enjoys an excellent plate of scrambled eggs and bacon and plenty of coffee. The eatery is almost certainly based on the Royal Café, a restaurant with a Swiss connection, judging by the 'Maison Suisse' sign that was displayed above its entrance. The restaurant survived into the 1960s, but after it closed down, the building was demolished, and now Atina House stands in its place. Conveniently, the underpass that takes visitors to the seafront where the statue of Ian Fleming may be seen is next to the site of the restaurant.

Port of Dover, Harbour House, Marine Parade, Dover, CT17 9BU
www.portofdover.com

That the James Bond of Ian Fleming's novels goes through the Port of Dover and takes a cross-Channel ferry to Calais is implied at the conclusion of *Moonraker*. In the aftermath of the explosion in the English Channel of the Moonraker atomic rocket, Bond and

Special Branch agent Gala Brand are ordered to leave the country until the crisis has blown over. Bond, certain that a romance with Brand is about to blossom, plans a getaway to France and orders the test driver of his new Bentley Mark VI – his 4½ litre having been wrecked by Drax – to drive down to Dover and get the car over to the ferry terminal at Calais, where Bond would meet him and the car. This suggests that the driver and Bond would cross by separate ferries.

In 1954, when the novel was written, the options for crossing the Channel were more limited than they are today, there being fewer sailings and fewer operators. Bond's driver would have taken a 'drive on and drive off' car ferry, at that time a fairly recent introduction to cross-Channel services; Dover's first state-of-the-art, purpose-built car ferry terminal had only been open since 1953. The Dover–Calais crossing was undertaken by the *Halladale*, a vessel operated by Townsend Brothers Ferries Ltd. Bond, on the other hand, probably intended to take the ferry train from London, hoping to travel with Gala Brand. Presumably wanting to sail to Calais, as opposed to Boulogne, Bond would have done well to take the 'Golden Arrow' service from London, which joined the ferry train boat, the *Côte d'Azur*, operated by the Société de Gérance et d'Armement, at Folkestone and sailed to Calais, the entire journey taking some seven hours, fifteen minutes. A question remains: why does Bond not take the air ferry, along with his car, from Ferryfield airport in Lydd in Kent, like he does in *Goldfinger*? The reason is that, when Fleming wrote *Moonraker* in the early months of 1954, Ferryfield had not yet been established. It would open later that year, with flights operated by Silver City Airways.

Bond returns to the Port of Dover in DIAMONDS ARE FOREVER. When diamond smuggler Peter Franks (Joe Robinson) rolls up at the port in his Triumph Stag, he is called into the customs office on some pretext, allowing Bond (Sean Connery) to slip into the driver's seat and take his place. With a false passport from Moneypenny (Lois Maxwell) and a promise to return with a tulip, Bond – now assuming the identity of Franks – moves off to board the Seaspeed hovercraft, the *Princess Margaret*. The vessel, which began service in 1968, operated between Dover and Boulogne, the implication being that the film, which cuts from the hovercraft to Amsterdam, denies us the chance to follow Bond's 400km or four-hour drive from Boulogne to the Dutch city.

Today, the hovercraft are no longer operating, ferries sail only to Calais, and the configuration of the port has changed, but the experience of preparing to cross the Channel, right down to that nervous moment when you wonder whether you will be stopped by the customs officers, remains the same as ever.

Bay Cottages, The Bay, St Margaret's Bay, Dover, CT15 6DY

Ian Fleming was a regular visitor to St Margaret's Bay since 1948, when his friend and neighbour in Jamaica, Noël Coward, invited Ian and Ann Rothermere (they were to marry in 1952) to stay at his house in Kent and escape unwanted attention as they conducted their affair. Noël had leased a row of six white-painted properties at the foot of the white cliffs and literally a stone's throw from the sea at the north end of the bay. He himself occupied the red-roofed building at the end of the row. Originally called 'Kay's Bluff', Noël named it 'White Cliffs'.

Fleming loved his visits there – apart from the setting, the cottages had a history that may also have attracted him; built in 1937, they had been used as a 'battle school' to train troops during the Second World War – and in 1951 gladly took over the lease of the adjacent property when its resident, thriller writer Eric Ambler, decided to move out. Fleming called his house 'Summer's Lease', and he and Ann would travel down from London over many weekends and a number of summers. The house offered them both a retreat and seclusion, but for Fleming the house also provided a convenient base for rounds of golf at Royal St George's in

Bay Cottages, St Margaret's Bay, Ian Fleming's coastal getaway.

Sandwich up the road, access to the sea (he set up a telescope to look out at the passing ships and the distant coast of France), and inspiration for his writing.

It is a sign of Fleming's affection for his beach house and the area that St Margaret's Bay would appear in two of his books. His third James Bond novel, *Moonraker*, is largely set around Deal a few miles to the north, and St Margaret's Bay is mentioned several times. Alas, 'Summer's Lease' does not make an appearance, but stumbling along the beach on the way to the Granville Hotel on the clifftop above the bay, having had a close shave when the cliffs above them are dynamited and the chalk tumbles around them, Bond and Special Branch agent Gala Brand would have walked past 'Summer's Lease'. In *Chitty Chitty Bang Bang*, Ian Fleming's children's novel, the eponymous car takes flight with the Pott family on board over Canterbury on its way to the Kent coast. Looking for somewhere to land for a picnic, the Potts notice that all the beaches – St Margaret's Bay, Walmer, Deal, Sandwich and Ramsgate – are crowded with families with the same idea.

The properties, now collectively called Bay Cottages, are private residences and not open to the public. One can, however, enjoy a day on the beach in front of them. Take the narrow and winding road from St Margaret's at Cliffe down to the seafront – take care of passing traffic and pedestrians – and once there, park in the car park provided. The cottages are a short walk along the shingle to the north-east.

The Granville, Hotel Road, St Margaret's Bay, Dover, CT15 6DX

After being almost crushed, in *Moonraker*, by a deliberately set-off cliff fall while relaxing on the beach below Sir Hugo Drax's rocket establishment near Deal, Bond and Special Branch agent Gala Brand stagger along the shingle towards St Margaret's Bay, outside Dover. At the seaside village, they climb the zigzagging path from the beach to the Granville Hotel, where they enjoy an hour's rest, a hot bath, several stiff brandies, and a meal of fried sole and Welsh rarebit.

Naturally, the Granville existed, and presumably Ian Fleming, who leased a cottage on the seafront, was a regular visitor. The hotel was built in 1882 and was developed and expanded in 1907. With its commanding, elevated position, and its multiple gables, white-painted walls, corner tower, and wooden veranda, the building was a distinctive landmark. At the time of Bond's visit, the three-star, twenty-three-bedroom establishment boasted fine dining with à la carte and table d'hote menus, a cocktail bar, luxurious rooms (not en suite – there were separate, communal bathrooms – but they did have wash basins), a billiard table, a tennis court, and, on a clear day and with the aid of a telescope, a sight of the town hall clock in Calais. Fried sole was a fixture on the menu, and diners could ask the chef to prepare any dish not listed, including Welsh rarebit.

By 1989, the hotel had closed its doors to guests. In 1994, it had formally ceased trading and was sold for development in February 1995. In March and August that year, the building was the target of arson attacks and was destroyed in the process. Today, the site is occupied by an apartment block, built in 1998. While there is nothing of the original remaining, the current building retains the name and, with its white-painted walls and multiple gables, offers a reasonable impression of the scale and appearance of the former hotel.

James Bond lovers can drive up to the front of the Granville on Hotel Road, and, for a Bondian experience that can still be enjoyed, walk up the path from the beach that leads to, and goes around, the former hotel. It is just about possible to peer over the dense vegetation and see the back of the building and the terrace where once guests played tennis.

St Margaret's Museum, Beach Road, St Margaret's Bay, Dover, CT15 6DZ

This small museum, run by the Bay Trust, includes displays about two of St Margaret's Bay's most famous residents, Noël Coward and, of course,

A private apartment building now stands in place of the Granville Hotel, St Margaret's Bay.

Ian Fleming. A statue of one of Ian Fleming's heroes, Winston Churchill, stands in the museum grounds. (The statue was destined for Trafalgar Square, but was rejected by Clementine Churchill, who thought the face too grumpy.) The museum is open all year round on Wednesdays to Sundays. Entry, via the Pines Garden Tea Room, is free.

The Royal St George's Golf Club, Sandwich, CT13 9PB
www.royalstgeorges.com

Ian Fleming was not the first writer to put a golf game into a spy thriller when he described the duel between James Bond and Goldfinger in his 1959 novel. There was before him, for example, E. Phillips Oppenheim, who, in his 1934 novel, *The Spy Paramount*, described a game of golf between the hero, freelance secret agent Major Martin Fawley, and the sinister Adolf Krust, a politician involved in the construction of a giant superweapon hidden in a mountain on the French–Italian border. What separates Fleming from the rest, however, is the quality of the writing. In a little over two chapters and across eighteen holes, Fleming keeps readers glued to the page with his intimate knowledge, precise detail, delicious dialogue, and taut prose. It says much about Fleming's writing that when the novel came to be filmed, the golf scenes were retained and formed a major sequence in the plot.

Being a lifelong golfer and living so close to Sandwich – he had homes at various times of his life at St Margaret's Bay, Sandwich Bay, and Bekesbourne, near Canterbury – Fleming was a regular visitor to the Royal St George's golf club. He not only played and socialised there, but in time he sat on the club's committee too. Tragically, Fleming died before he could take up his duties as club captain, a long-coveted position. In 1959, the club provided the inspiration for the epic golf match between Bond and Goldfinger, held at the Royal St Marks in Sandwich, which is the Royal St George's in all but name.

The club is open to non-members to visit, but to play a round of golf, players must be able to demonstrate a handicap of 18.4 or less. This would not have worried Bond, who, like his creator, has a handicap of nine.

Lydd, London Ashford Airport, Romney Marsh, TN29 9QL
www.lydd-airport.co.uk

Before Concorde, the most exciting flight that jetsetters and sunseekers could take in Britain was the air ferry, which, in its heyday during the 1950s and 1960s, flew passengers and their vehicles across the Channel from Lydd Airport, known as Ferryfield, to the glamour spots of Europe. Passengers, waiting for their vehicles to be driven on to the aircraft could relax in the reception lounge, pop to the shop, change currency at the on-site bank, or sip a cocktail in the licensed bar and restaurant. The airport owners were keen to attract non-flyers too, making Ferryfield available for wedding receptions, functions, and dinner dances. James Bond uses the service in the novel of *Goldfinger*. He follows Goldfinger's gold-laden Rolls-Royce to the airport, and, with the help of the customs officers, plants a homing device on the car. He observes the car being loaded into the nose of the Bristol Superfreighter and the aircraft taking off towards Le Touquet, safe in the knowledge that he can track the car, have a relaxing lunch, and catch a later flight.

In 1958, when Ian Fleming wrote the novel, the cross-Channel service between Lydd and Le Touquet was just four years old. Silver City Airways operated its inaugural passenger flight in July 1954. Before then, services flew from nearby Lympne but were frequently disrupted by bad weather. For much of the 1950s, the service flew to the gaming and beach resort of Le Touquet only, but it expanded, and by the early 1960s, the service, now operated by British United Air Ferries, took passengers to Basle, Strasbourg and Liege, among other cities. In March 1964, the air ferry began its run to Geneva, which was fortunate for the film-makers of GOLDFINGER, because it meant that Goldfinger could fly directly to Switzerland, rather than drive through France to Geneva, as he does in the novel.

In the film, Goldfinger (Gert Fröbe), followed by Bond (Sean Connery), who, with his Aston Martin DB5, again takes a later flight, travels on an ATL-98 Carvair, a converted Douglas DC-4. There was an element of trickery here, because the Ferryfield sequence was filmed at Southend Airport in Essex. That is not to say, however, that the DB5 never had its tyres on the Lydd tarmac. In February 1965, the *Kentish Express* reported that the vehicle – a publicity model, if not the car seen in the film – had returned to the UK after a tour of the USA and Europe to promote the film, flying into Lydd from Le Touquet. The driver was one Mike Ashley, a sales rep with Aston Martin.

The airport still operates today, but the commercial flights to Europe have long ceased. Those who wish to follow in Bond's footsteps, however, may charter a flight to Le Touquet, and, while not as glamorous as the former restaurant that once served Continental-style table d'hote and à la carte menus, take refreshments at the airport café.

OXFORDSHIRE

Blenheim Palace, Woodstock, OX20 1PS
www.blenheimpalace.com

Ian Fleming might have been amused to learn that Blenheim Place, the birthplace of his hero Sir Winston

Churchill, doubled in SPECTRE as a meeting place in Rome for Spectre agents and assassins and provided the backdrop to the scene where Bond (Daniel Craig) is dramatically reacquainted with his stepbrother, Franz Oberhauser (Christoph Waltz), who later reveals himself to be Ernst Stavro Blofeld.

In the film, Bond pulls his Aston Martin DB10 into a courtyard defined by grand, Italianate buildings. This is the Great Court, which was built in the early eighteenth-century Neo-classical style of English Baroque. Getting out of his car, which is somewhat overshadowed by the host of Spectre supercars already parked up, Bond walks towards one of the flanking, colonnaded blocks. This is the front of Stable Court; the opposite frontage of Kitchen Court can be seen behind him. Later in the sequence, as he makes his escape, having rejoined his vehicle and with

Blenheim Palace (pictured here at Christmas), birthplace of Sir Winston Churchill and a SPECTRE meeting place.

Hinx (Dave Bautista) in pursuit in a Jaguar CX75, Bond speeds through the archway into Stable Court and, thanks to the magic of cinema, on to the streets of Rome.

Soldiers of Oxfordshire Museum, Park Street, Woodstock, OX20 1SN
www.sofo.org.uk

The Soldiers of Oxfordshire Museum tells the story of two Oxfordshire regiments, the Oxfordshire and Buckinghamshire Light Infantry and the Queen's Own Oxfordshire Hussars. The latter was the regiment in which Valentine Fleming, Ian's father, served. Valentine had enlisted in the yeomanry regiment by the time he had been elected Conservative member of parliament for the Henley Division of South Oxfordshire in 1910. He was in good company; his friend and fellow officer in the Hussars was Winston Churchill. Just four years later, Britain was at war, and in August 1914 the regiment headed to Flanders on the Western Front. Tragically, Major Valentine Fleming was killed in May 1917 while in command of a squadron of Hussars who were defending their position at Gillemont Farm against two companies of German infantry.

The Soldiers of Oxfordshire Museum, which is situated in the grounds of the Oxfordshire Museum, has a display about Valentine Fleming's role in the Queen's Own Oxfordshire Hussars, and his sons, including Ian, are mentioned too.

Braziers Park, Ipsden, Wallingford, OX10 6AN
www.braziers.org.uk

Ian Fleming spent his earliest years at Braziers Park, a modest mansion near the village of Ipsden in south Oxfordshire. His parents, Valentine and Evelyn, bought the property in 1906 and lived there until 1914. Ian, born in 1908, would spend six years there. The house was built in the Jacobean style in 1688 but was transformed into a Gothic-style mock castle at the end of the eighteenth century. More building work was ordered by Valentine, who added a west wing, but he retained the Gothic style. Architectural historian Nikolaus Pevsner thought the house more sombre than elegant, though he admired its symmetry.

Braziers Park is best reached from the A4074, the road that runs between Oxford and Reading. The house is signposted about 15km north of Reading and is located off to the east at the end of a narrow lane. The house is not open to the public, but it is run as a residential college that offers courses on well-being and spirituality, and it is home to a community that maintains the house and the farm. There are open days and festivals at the house every so often, which may provide the best opportunity to visit Ian Fleming's childhood home.

Braziers Park, childhood home of Ian Fleming.

Cooper's Marmalade Factory (site of), 27 Park End Street, Oxford, OX1 1HU; 110–120 Botley Road, OX2 0HH
At home, while resting between missions, Bond is a creature of habit. As revealed in *From Russia With Love*, breakfast consists of a single boiled egg, and two slices of wholewheat toast with Jersey butter, Tiptree Little Scarlet strawberry jam, and Cooper's Vintage Oxford marmalade. As the name suggests, the last was a product of Oxford. It was made in the Cooper's jam and marmalade factory on Botley Road at a location that is today occupied by a Waitrose supermarket. Cooper's first purpose-made factory, which had ceased production only a few years before *From Russia With Love* was published in 1957, was in Park End Street. The building still stands and is of significant architectural interest, the main offices being red brick with Bath stone dressings and decorated with orange fruit and foliage, and the site of the factory at the rear retaining the

The site of Cooper's marmalade factory, Oxford.

structures where the fruit was boiled. The building is easy to visit, being opposite Oxford railway station.

Ashmolean Museum, Beaumont Street, Oxford, OX1 2PH
www.ashmolean.org

In 1978 and 1979, Ann Fleming presented to the Ashmolean Museum a collection of antiquities that her and Ian's son Caspar had assembled in his teenage years and during his short time at Oxford University. The items reflect Caspar's wide interest in the archaeology of Europe and include Bronze Age swords and socketed axes, an Iron Age torc, and Byzantine amulets. Almost all the objects remain in the museum's stores, but several items are on display. In the 'Mediterranean World' gallery, there is a pendant with the Virgin and Child (look for the museum's accession number of AN1978.67 on the caption underneath or beside the object in the display cabinet), another pendant with a depiction of St Nicholas (AN1978.96), a seal with a small bust of Christ (AN1978.74), and a gold strap-end (AN1978.30), all dating between the fourth and seventh centuries. In the 'England 400–1600' gallery, visitors may find two Visigothic buckles of fifth to ninth century ad date (AN1978.28 and AN1978.29).

Pitt Rivers Museum, Parks Road, Oxford, OX1 3PP

www.prm.ox.ac.uk

No sightseeing trip in Oxford is complete without a visit to the Pitt Rivers Museum of anthropology and world archaeology, an institution whose relatively small space belies the enormous number and variety of objects crammed in its cases and drawers. The museum has on display several objects to interest the James Bond lover. A case on the ground floor devoted to masks includes Japanese Noh masks similar to that worn by Lyutsifer Safin (Rami Malek) in NO TIME TO DIE. The first floor has skiing equipment that will bring to mind Bond's adventures in the snow in the book and film of *On Her Majesty's Secret Service*. The second floor is devoted to weapons, and in one of the cases there is a Beretta M1934 and Walther PP, both accompanied by labels that allude to James Bond. Enter the museum through the Natural History Museum on Parks Road.

New College, Holywell Street, Oxford, OX1 3BN

www.new.ox.ac.uk

Bond must have had difficulty deciding who to root for in the annual Boat Race, being an alumnus of both Oxford and Cambridge. In YOU ONLY LIVE TWICE, we learn that Bond (Sean Connery) took a first in Oriental languages at Cambridge University. In TOMORROW NEVER DIES, Bond (Pierce Brosnan) is at Oxford University, brushing up on a little Danish. After an establishing shot of a college building, we see Bond in the language tutor's room (Cecilie Thomsen), in the throes of conjugation.

The establishing shot shows the Holywell Quadrangle and the wing of buildings that line Holywell Street. On the right-hand side of the shot, one can just make out Robinson Tower, which forms the main entrance into the college. While the public is permitted to visit the college – visitors are directed to the original college entrance in New College Lane – access to college buildings is restricted and it may not be possible to visit the Holywell Quadrangle. However, the college porters at the New College Lane and Holywell Street entrances are friendly and knowledgeable, and they may be able to help not only with access but also reveal some secrets about the filming. In addition, the college offers bed-and-breakfast accommodation, which gives visitors further access to college buildings. When visiting, do look round the Cloisters. It will be familiar to Harry Potter fans as a location for scenes in *Harry Potter and the Goblet of Fire*, but there are also fascinating inscriptions around the walls memorialising past alumni and fellows, including Hugh Gaitskell, leader of the Labour Party between 1955 and 1963 and lover of Ann Fleming.

New College has another Fleming connection. It is the college that Ian's son Caspar attended from 1971. He initially went up to read English, but he transferred to Egyptian and Assyrian studies, allowing him to pursue his interest in archaeology, antiquities and Egyptology. Despite his devotion to the subject and his having the potential to become an authority on archaeology, Caspar's mental health issues were severe and he dropped out after two years.

Aston Martin Heritage Trust, Drayton St Leonards, Wallingford, OX10 7BG
amht.org.uk

This small museum, run by the Aston Martin Heritage Trust, is located in the tiny village of Drayton St Leonard, near Wallingford, and housed in a

Holywell Quadrangle, New College, Oxford, a college with Fleming and Bond connections.

magnificent medieval barn (itself worth the admission fee) built for the monks of Dorchester Abbey. The cars on display change from time to time, but vehicles have included a 1972 Aston Martin DB5, a prototype of the Vanquish (the model that appeared in DIE ANOTHER DAY), a Nimrod/ Aston Martin racing car, which tore around Le Mans in 1982, and a full-scale ceramic and plastic model of the exclusive Aston Martin One-77, of which just seventy-seven were built. There were more treasures around the edges of the barn. Display cases of trophies, medals and flags highlight Aston Martin's many successes on the racetrack. Another case celebrates its drivers, among them the legendary Sir Stirling Moss (who takes his place in Bond lore as a character in one of Ian Fleming's unused television series treatments, 'Murder on Wheels', which was incorporated into Anthony Horowitz's 2015 Bond novel, *Trigger Mortis*). Seeing the helmet and overalls worn by Moss during his time driving for Aston Martin will be a thrill to any motoring enthusiast. No collection of Aston Martin memorabilia is complete without reference to James Bond, and naturally part of another display case is devoted to toy cars, models, and other representations of 007's cars.

Huntercombe Golf Club, Nuffield, Henley-on-Thames, RG9 5SL
www.huntercombegolfclub.co.uk

Ian Fleming's love of golf began at an early age. He first picked up a set of clubs aged about 6 while at Durnford School, and his interest in the game was nurtured by his grandmother,

Huntercombe golf course, a regular haunt for both Ian Fleming and James Bond.

Kate Fleming, who played regularly at her local course at Huntercombe. The young Ian, who eschewed shooting and other country sports beloved by his brother Peter, would accompany his grandmother around the course. Eventually, aged 15, he learned to play seriously. Until the Second World War, Ian played frequently at Huntercombe, and well into his 20s, he would return to Joyce Grove, his grandparents' estate in Nettlebed, at weekends and play a few rounds at the course. Bond is also familiar with the course. In *Goldfinger*, we learn that he plays his golf close to London and headquarters, including, notably, at Huntercombe.

The golf club is open to members and non-members alike. Bond lovers who are not quite as keen on golf as 007 or Fleming may prefer to explore the greens and fairways using the various public footpaths that cross the course.

Joyce Grove, Nettlebed, Henley-on-Thames, RG9 5DF

Joyce Grove was the home of Ian Fleming's grandparents, Robert and Kate Fleming. The original late seventeenth-century house of Joyce Grove was demolished by Robert when he acquired the estate of Nettlebed Manor in 1903, and a new Gothic-style mansion was erected in its place by the following year. Robert was, briefly, lord of the manor, his new house being the manor house until he relinquished his rights over Nettlebed Common in 1906. In practical terms, however, Robert retained his lordly interest in the affairs of the village. His estate offered work for many of the villagers, and he provided the village with a new cricket pavilion and working men's club or village hall. But just as the lord giveth, he could also taketh away: Robert shut down the Red Lion public house because its patrons were making too much noise.

Naturally, the young Ian Fleming was a regular visitor at Joyce Grove, and for a time after the death of his father, Valentine, in 1917 during the First World War, he and his brothers had the run of a wing of the house during weekends. Ian continued to visit the house into his adulthood, and he would use it as a base when playing golf at nearby Huntercombe or entertain golfers and bridge players in the house. Robert died in 1933, and the estate passed to his widow Kate. On her death in 1937, the estate went to Robert's surviving sons. The house was then given to St Mary's Hospital, Paddington, and subsequently became a nursing home, a role that it continued until 2020 as a hospice run by the Sue Ryder charity. The estate was subsequently acquired for the development of houses and apartments.

The house itself is a red brick and Bath stone mansion on the edge of Nettlebed, a village located between the small towns of Wallingford and Henley-on-Thames. Architectural historian Nikolaus Pevsner described Joyce Grove as a mansion in dull Jacobean style. From the outside, the house bears little obvious indication of once being occupied by the Flemings, but there are subtle signs. The family crest is shown in relief on the front elevation of the house, with its distinctive goat emblem and well-known motto, 'Let the deed shaw', and the inscription, 'R.1904.F' (RF = Robert Fleming), recording the completion of the remodelling, is carved into the stone above a window looking out to the terrace. While Joyce Grove is not generally accessible to the public, it is possible to look down a gravelled, (evergreen) tree-lined approach to the house from the side gateway of wrought iron and stone finials that faces the main road (High Street) through the village. While standing at the side gateway, turn to face the main road. The row of houses to the left includes the site of the former Red Lion.

As with many of his experiences, Ian Fleming's time at Joyce Grove seeped into the world of James Bond. In *Goldfinger*, Fleming describes Auric Goldfinger's house, The Grange, which is located near Reculver in Kent, as a turn-of-the-century mansion with a gravel sweep in front. He notes that its drive is bordered by high evergreens, and that the adjoining stabling and garages have become Goldfinger's gold-processing factory. In the descriptions of the drive, the house and stables, Fleming was describing the house he knew as a child.

Joyce Grove, Nettlebed, home of Ian Fleming's grandparents.

St Bartholomew's Church, Port Hill, Nettlebed, Henley-on-Thames, RG9 5RL
Like St James's Church in Sevenhampton in Wiltshire, St Bartholomew's Church in Nettlebed deserves to be a place of pilgrimage for Bond lovers. Several generations of Flemings are buried in its graveyard, and exploring other parts of the church reveals further connections to the family. Inside the lychgate at the beginning of the path through the churchyard from the main road, Valentine Fleming is commemorated in a dedication to the fallen of the First World War. Opposite the inscription is another dedicated to the fallen of the Second World War, which records the name of Michael Fleming, one of Ian's brothers. Within the churchyard, in a row furthest from the church, there are the simple headstones marking the graves of Ian's brother Peter (his headstone including a self-penned epitaph), Peter's wife Celia Johnson, Peter's son Nichol, Ian's mother Evelyn, Michael's son David, and Ian's half-sister, Amaryllis. Not far away is the

St Bartholomew's Church, burial place of Ian Fleming's parents, grandparents and brothers.

larger, but only slightly more ornate, burial plot of Ian's grandparents, Robert and Kate.

The lives of the Flemings are further commemorated inside the church. The wall along the north aisle includes a stained-glass window depicting the saints Valentine and St Michael to honour Valentine and Michael's wartime sacrifices, and there are separate inscriptions on the wall dedicated to them as well. On the opposite wall, another stained-glass window and inscription serve as a memorial to Peter Fleming. The window, a remarkable work of craftmanship and art by John Piper, contains motifs that allude to Peter's career as a writer and traveller.

Nettlebed Club, 32 High Street, Nettlebed, Henley-on-Thames, RG9 5DD

If you walk along the High Street, you will pass the Nettlebed Village Club, on the north side of the road. This was built in 1913 with funds provided by Robert Fleming, Ian Fleming's grandfather. The Old School House is almost opposite on the other side of the road. The wall facing the main road carries a plaque erected in memory of Peter Fleming – Ian's elder brother – and Philip Fleming – Ian's uncle. The inscription commemorates 'their affection for the village of Nettlebed to which they contributed so much'. Ian Fleming made less of a mark on the village, but it does achieve the accolade of being mentioned in a Bond novel. In *The Spy Who Loved Me*, heroine Vivienne Michel's first boyfriend, Derek, gives a false Nettlebed address to the manager of the Royalty Kinema in Windsor, who catches Derek and Vivienne in a compromising position in the back seats of the auditorium.

Greys Court, Rotherfield Greys, Henley-on-Thames, RG9 4PG

www.nationaltrust.org.uk

Greys Court, 4 miles south-east of Nettlebed, was for a short time the home of Ian Fleming's mother, Evelyn. She bought the late sixteenth-century house in 1935, intending it to be both a home for her, and a place where Peter Fleming, Ian's brother, could write. Evelyn immediately made alterations to the house, particularly to the entrance hall, and began preparing the Cromwellian Stables for Peter. When Peter married Celia Johnson, however, it was evident that he would not require the use of the house. Just two years later, Greys Court was sold to the Brunner family.

Greys Court is a National Trust property and open to the public. Visitors can take a tour around various parts of the house, including the dining room, the bedrooms, the library, and the kitchen, and enter the Cromwellian Stables on the other side of Green Court, the lawn that separates the buildings. Most of Evelyn's

Greys Court, near Henley-on-Thames, home briefly to Ian Fleming's mother, Evelyn.

modifications have been removed, but a spiral staircase that she put in can still be seen.

White Pond Farm, Balhams's Lane, Stonor, Henley-on-Thames, RG9 6HG
www.whitepondfarm.co.uk

Being a milkman can be a risky business. That is certainly the case in THE LIVING DAYLIGHTS, when Necros (Andreas Wisniewski) garrottes an unsuspecting milkman making his rounds at a farmhouse. Necros pulls the struggling milkman over the farm wall and takes his place, allowing him to infiltrate the nearby MI6 safehouse of Blayden.

The scene was filmed at White Pond Farm on the junction of Balham's Lane and the B480 at Stonor, close to Stonor Park, which doubled for Blayden. The film-makers made very little alteration to the exterior of the farm, and the farm entrance and outside wall that faces the road are today near-identical to how they appear on screen. The setting can, of course, be seen from the public road, but some of the buildings within the farm are available to hire as holiday

White Pond Farm, Stonor: scene of a milkman's delivery of death in THE LIVING DAYLIGHTS.

cottages and make an appropriate base for exploring the Bond locations, both literary and cinematic, in the area.

Stonor Park, Henley-on-Thames, RG9 6HF
www.stonor.com

The house and grounds of Stonor Park were used extensively in THE LIVING DAYLIGHTS as the MI6 safehouse, Blayden. Following his extraction from Bratislava with the help of Bond (Timothy Dalton), General Georgi Koskov (Jeroen Krabbé) is taken to Blayden to be debriefed by M (Robert Brown) and the Minister of Defence (Geoffrey Keen), with Bond arriving later with caviar and other luxury food from Harrods. After Bond, M and the Minister of Defence return to London, Necros (Andreas Wisniewski), an assassin working for arms dealer Brad Whittaker (Joe Don Baker), having made it through the security checkpoints by disguising himself as a milkman, causes mayhem by letting off milk bottle-shaped grenades, and in the ensuing chaos kidnaps Koskov and makes his escape by helicopter.

The magnificent exteriors of the house at Stonor and its surrounding landscape are rewarded in the film with some major screentime. We see Bond drive up to the front of the house in an Aston Martin V8 Volante and then walk, Harrods hamper in hand, to the front door; the Chapel of the Holy Trinity is in the background. The security gate where Necros, getting out of his Unigate milk float, is frisked by MI6 guards utilises the two late eighteenth-century, brick-built piers topped by stone ball finials that flank the approach to the house. The small guardhouse was a temporary structure erected for the film, while the fence that extended from the piers has since been removed. The security gate is seen again when a fire engine and ambulance arrive following the explosions. Necros pulls into a small courtyard and delivers the milk at the back door of the kitchen. While the kitchen interiors were created in the studio, the sequence reflects

Stonor Park was a major location in THE LIVING DAYLIGHTS.

the layout of the house, as in reality Stonor's medieval kitchen is located off this small courtyard.

Stonor Park, which had its origins in the thirteenth century, but was extensively remodelled in the seventeenth and eighteenth centuries, is open to the public and a must-visit for Bond lovers, who can explore the grounds and recreate some of the exciting moments and views from the Blayden sequence. Do also explore the house itself, which has been the home of the Stonor family for generations. While the interiors were not used for the film, there is a small display in the house recalling the time that Bond visited. Look out as well for a display showing photographs of Ralph Stonor's (the fifth Lord Camoys) service in the Queen's Own Oxfordshire Hussars in the early twentieth century. This was the regiment in which Ian Fleming's father, Valentine, also served.

SURREY

Enton Hall, Enton, Godalming, GU8 5AW
In 1956, Ian Fleming entered Enton Hall, a health farm near Godalming in Surrey, for a course of naturopathic treatment. His wife Ann had visited the clinic earlier in January that year and would be a regular guest. Fleming did not take his treatment seriously, and often escaped the grounds of the hall. Nevertheless, his stay had sufficient impact on him to provide the inspiration for Shrublands, the health farm that Bond visits in *Thunderball*.

Enton Hall was built in 1881 for the Eastwood family and was later owned by Lord Chichester, who brought in renowned horticulturist Gertrude Jekyll to design an ornamental garden and provide advice on the neat terraces and lawns lined with conifers and shrubberies. The buildings were set within a vast estate of woodland and farmland, and the entrance to the hall was guarded by a lodge and approached by a narrow, leafy lane through gently undulating countryside. This peaceful, tucked-away place was ideal for R. Atkinson Reddell, an osteopath who was looking to establish a health farm. He bought the estate in 1948, and a year later, after altering the hall to include thirty-three bedrooms, and building nineteen chalets and nine staff cottages, he opened the Enton Hall Heath Hydro, a residential clinic and health farm devoted to, as the promotional literature put it, 'the

The gate and lodge of Enton Hall, inspiration for Shrublands.

renewal and preservation of health by natural biological methods'. The health farm admitted its last guest in 1988, and the hall was sold and converted into private luxury apartments.

Readers of *Thunderball* who had been guests at Enton Hall would have found the description of the fictional Shrublands very familiar. In the book, Bond is met by a taxi sent by the clinic. Enton Hall similarly sent taxis to collect guests from the local railway station at Witley, and no doubt Fleming used this service. As his taxi enters the grounds of Shrublands, set, as is Enton Hall, in quiet countryside, Bond notes the imposing, mock-battlemented gateway, a description that applies equally well to Enton Hall's porte-cochère through which vehicles passed. Approaching the main house, a red-brick Victorian building, Bond spots the glass sun parlour, which extends from the building to the edge of the lawn. The description matches Enton Hall, which is also a red-brick Victorian building with a south-facing sun lounge overlooking an extensive terraced lawn. Bond is shown to 'the Annex', where bedrooms are named after flowers and shrubs, and indeed an annex at Enton Hall was called the Oak House. Bedrooms at the time of Fleming's visit were equipped with their own hot and cold running water, central heating, telephones and radio. Treatment rooms at Enton Hall also matched those described at Shrublands, right down to the compartments divided by plastic curtains. At one point, Bond sits at a little café-style table overlooking the lawn and consumes hot vegetable soup. The scene replicates an image in Enton Hall's brochure, 'View from sun lounge', which shows two men at a little café table at the window overlooking the lawn. According to a price list contemporary with Fleming's visit, guests staying in the annex at Enton Hall were charged 22 guineas a week (about £23), a figure close to the £20 for a week's stay that Bond's taxi driver mentions.

Fleming looked to his experiences at Enton Hall when he came to describe events at Shrublands in *Thunderball*. Bond lovers cannot ordinarily visit the site of Enton Hall, but they can stop at the estate's entrance on Water Lane between the villages of Witley and Enton and imagine a dyspeptic Ian Fleming arriving in a taxi and continuing up the drive.

The National Shooting Centre, Bisley, Surrey, GU24 0PB
nationalshootingcentre.co.uk

The short story 'The Living Daylights', part of the *Octopussy* volume, begins at the shooting ranges at Bisley. As usual, Ian Fleming accurately describes the scene; the landmarks he mentions in the story – among them the Century Range, the clock tower, and the gun club pavilion – are all there at Bisley. The

600-yard Century Range opens out from the north-east edge of the complex, while the clock tower stands some distance to its west. In between is the Bisley Gun Club pavilion. The story was adapted fairly faithfully for the film THE LIVING DAYLIGHTS, and even Bisley gets a nod in the form of the shooting gallery in Vienna's Wurstelprater amusement park, where Bond's (Timothy Dalton) outstanding form threatens to wipe out the owner's stock of cheap soft toys.

Today, the range is home to several shooting clubs and organisations and is open to the public for target and clay shooting. Anyone wishing to try their hand on Century Range and attempt to match Bond's impressive performance can book a target shooting session with the National Shooting Centre. Head to the centre's website for more details.

SUSSEX

The Frankland Arms, 3 London Road, Washington, RH20 4AL
thefranklandarms.com

After a spell at Shrublands health farm near the village of Washington in Sussex in *Thunderball*, James Bond is a changed man. Not only does he feel healthier and full of energy, but he is also drinking tea, a beverage that he had abhorred. During his treatment, he visits the tea rooms and cafés of Washington – the Rose Cottage, the Thatched Barn, and the Transport Café – where he finds that tea with sugar is as intoxicating as champagne.

At the time Ian Fleming was writing, there were several tea rooms in the village, including the Settatrees Tea Rooms and the Clematis Tea Rooms, and there was a transport café – Bridge Café – just up the road in the neighbouring village of Ashington. Those have long disappeared, but the Frankland Arms, which also existed in Fleming's time, has survived and is a good option for anyone seeking refreshment in the village.

Amberley Museum, New Barn Road, Amberley, Arundel, BN18 9LT
www.amberleymuseum.co.uk

During the filming of A VIEW TO A KILL, part of West Sussex was transformed into part of northern California when Amberley Museum, the site of a former chalk quarry in the South Downs, provided the setting for villain Max Zorin's mining operations near San Francisco. Several scenes that appear in the film's exciting climax were filmed here, and the chalk quarries and kilns that doubled as Zorin's Main Strike Mine can be seen today within the open-air museum. In the film, industrialist Max Zorin (Christopher Walken) is planning to set off a mass of explosives in a disused silver mine at a vulnerable point of the San Andreas Fault in order to trigger an earthquake, causing Silicon Valley to be destroyed and allowing Zorin Industries to control the world's microchip market.

The entrance of the Main Strike Mine appears in several scenes, most dramatically when Zorin's bodyguard and enforcer May Day (Grace Jones) has a change of heart after discovering that Zorin has betrayed her. She emerges from the mine steering a rail handcar that carries the detonator. Alas, the brake is faulty, and she must keep hold of it so that she can take the detonator out of harm's way before it explodes. The mine entrance is located at the furthest end of the museum close to Brockham, a little station that forms part of the museum's on-site narrow-gauge railway; what in fact served as the mine entrance is the opening of a tunnel that leads to another quarry. There is no public access into the tunnel, but visitors can gain good views of the entrance from several vantage points. Helpfully, the location is marked as 'Mainstrike Mine' on the museum's visitor map.

The entrance to Main Strike Mine at Amberley Museum.

The Railway Exhibition Hall close to the mine entrance is dedicated to narrow-gauge railways and houses locomotives, rail carts, carriages and other rail machinery and equipment. Among the exhibits is a skip or hopper in which Bond (Roger Moore) and Stacey Sutton (Tanya Roberts) hide, allowing them to sneak into the mine and view Zorin's operations. The skip on display retains the Zorin branding, having been painted green and carrying the black 'Z' logo. None of the skips that appear in the film were originally used at the quarries but were brought from Basingstoke Canal and had before that been used by Southern Water. More rolling stock seen in the film can be found at Brockham station. There visitors will see one of the rail carts that was used to transport Zorin's mineworkers into the mine. Though now badly flaking, the green paintwork of Zorin Industries still survives.

Turning back towards the museum entrance, visitors pass the De Witt kilns, a group of impressive brick-built lime kilns erected in 1905. The top of the

One of the carriages that transported Max Zorin's men into Main Strike Mine in A VIEW TO A KILL.

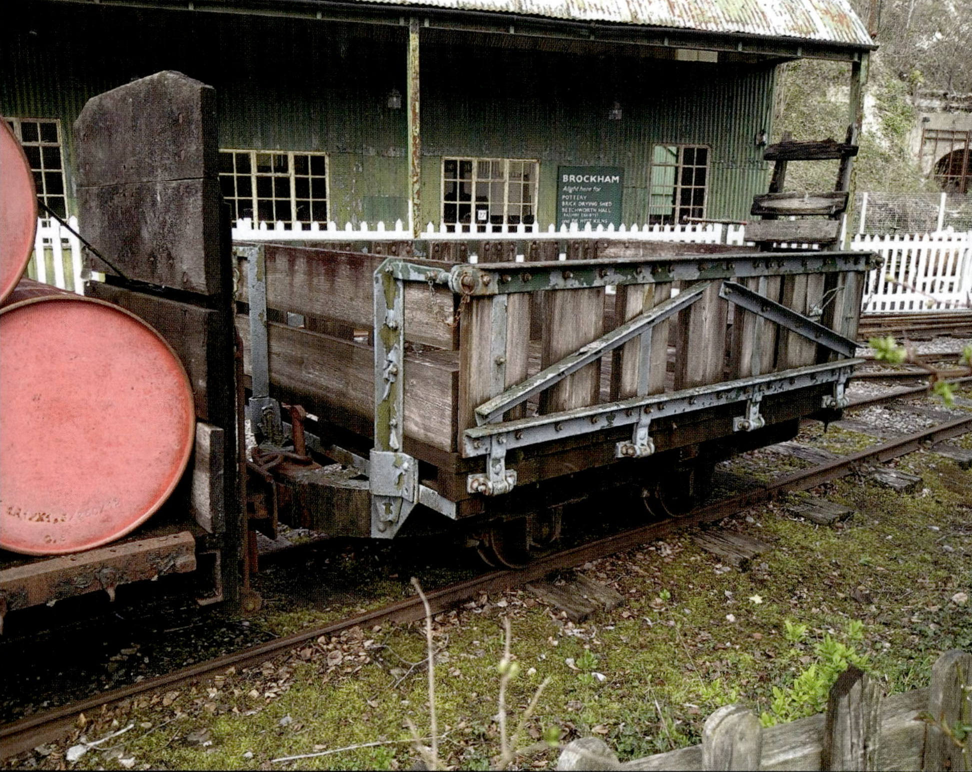

chimneys, which can be reached via a walkway, doubled in A VIEW TO A KILL as an access point to the mine, and in the film, Stacey is seen clambering out of one of the chimneys. She is then spotted by Zorin, who is hovering over Main Strike Mine in an airship. The airship descends and henchman Scarpine grabs Stacey. This scene was filmed close to the museum's Southdown bus garage. Returning to the museum entrance, visitors will see signs for the White Pit and the Paviors' Museum of Roadmaking. It was in this area that Zorin's on-site office was set up.

Amberley Museum is a treat for Bond lovers. Not only does it offer them the chance to see and interact with key film locations, but it also provides a fun experience for all the family, with some amazing history on display and lots of activities for visitors young and old to enjoy. What is more, the staff are very knowledgeable and are all too happy to reveal more about the time when James Bond came to the museum.

ON THE ROAD WITH JAMES BOND

In addition to the many exciting locations mentioned in the Bond novels, Ian Fleming includes some thrilling car journeys taken by 007 or other characters. These are invariably described in such detail that it is possible for Bond lovers to map the routes precisely and experience the journeys for themselves. Two of the journeys – contained within the novels of *Moonraker* and *Goldfinger* – are set in England and give us a passenger-side view of Bond's routes from London to the coast of Kent, one via the A20 road to Sir Hugo Drax's Moonraker research facility between Dover and Deal, the other via the A2 road to Auric Goldfinger's metallurgical establishment near Ramsgate. While the journeys are not perhaps as glamorous as Bond's epic motoring from Le Touquet to Geneva, also in *Goldfinger*, or as perilous as Vivienne Michel's road trip on a Vespa to the Adirondacks in New York State in *The Spy Who Loved Me*, they are nevertheless exhilarating to read and offer insights into Bond's world and the changing landscape.

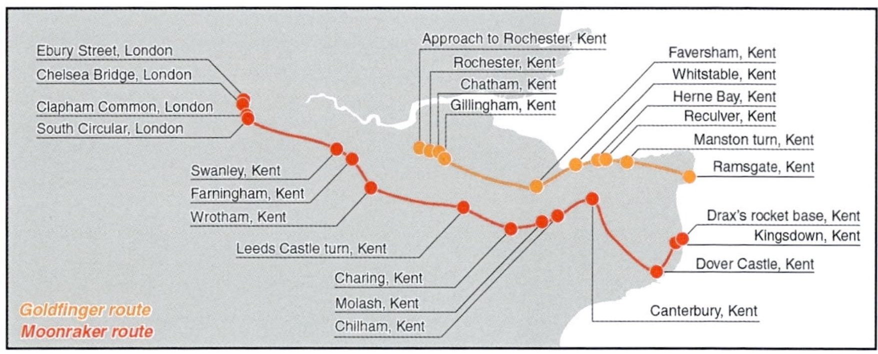

***Bond's routes through Kent, as described in* Moonraker *and* Goldfinger.**

London to Dover

To reconstruct Bond's typical route from London to Dover, we need to combine two separate journeys described in *Moonraker*. One is Bond's first – and relatively leisurely – trip down to Drax's research facility between Dover and Deal following a briefing by M and meetings with Assistant Commissioner Vallance at Scotland Yard and Professor Train at the Ministry of Supply. The second is a rather more furious drive pursuing Drax from Drax's residence on Ebury Street to Charing Hill, where Bond is stopped prematurely. For the route between London and Maidstone, we need to start with the later journey.

Beginning at the eastern end of **Ebury Street**, Bond follows Drax's white Mercedes 300 S in his Bentley 4½-litre coupé to **Chelsea Bridge**. The route between these two points is not specified, but it is reasonable to suggest that Bond drives west along Ebury Street, into Pimlico Road (A3214), and turns left towards the south on to Chelsea Bridge Road (A3216). Alternatively, from Ebury Street, he drives on to Buckingham Palace Road and then into Ebury Bridge Road to join Chelsea Bridge Road. From Chelsea Bridge, he follows Drax to the edge of **Clapham Common**. To get there, Bond would have continued south on the A3216 after the bridge along Victoria Road, passing Battersea Power Station on his left and Battersea Park on his right. When the A3216 crosses Battersea Park Road, it becomes Queenstown Road and then Cedars Road when it crosses the junction with Lavender Hill and Wandsworth Road. Bond would have continued along the A3216 until it met the northern edge of Clapham Common. By now, Bond has figured out Drax's route and knows that he will take the **South Circular Road** (A205) and connect with the A20 road that will take him through Kent. To join the South Circular would have required Bond to perform a dog-leg, first turning right at the junction with Cedars Road (A3216) and Clapham Common North Side (A3) and then left into The Avenue (A205), taking Bond through the common. Now on the South Circular Road, Bond would have continued along the road, through Tulse Hill, Dulwich, Forest Hill and Catford. At Horn Park, at the junction of Westhorne Avenue (A205) and Sidcup Road (A20), Fleming tells us that Bond swung round the roundabout there to turn right (taking the third exit) into the A20, reaching 40mph and his tyres screeching. Today, this leg of the journey will take ordinary drivers the best part of an hour to complete. It would have taken Bond a considerably shorter time, given the lighter traffic and the high speeds he would have been able to maintain.

The A20 provides easier driving for Bond. He puts on his driving goggles in anticipation of some fast motoring and, having bypassed Sidcup and driven through Foots Cray, is soon accelerating through **Swanley Junction**. Since Bond's journey, the Sidcup bypass has been extended to bypass Foots Cray. To get back on to Bond's route, leave the bypass at the junction of the A20 with Edgington Way (A223) and turn right at the next roundabout to join Maidstone Road. (Edgington Way and Maidstone Road preserve the original route of the A20.) Continue along Maidstone Road – which becomes London Road – into Swanley.

The commuter town of Swanley was, when Ian Fleming was writing, known as Swanley Junction. Then it consisted of little more than a few houses, a nursery and orchards, a jam factory, and a hospital that had developed at a railway junction established with the creation of a station in 1861 near the crossroads where the A20 met Swanley Lane and Station Road/Goldsel Road. Bond would have continued south-east through the town on London Road and into the High Street and thereafter continue towards Farningham, but today it is not possible to follow Bond's route precisely, as London Road in the centre of Swanley has been pedestrianised. Instead, drivers are required to loop around the town centre on the B2173 and rejoin the

***The road through Swanley Junction – now simply Swanley – towards Farningham that Bond takes on his way to the Kent coast in* Moonraker.**

former line of the A20 at the High Street (the current A20 bypassing Swanley to the south-west), which, a little further on, once again becomes London Road. Bond lovers who wish to trace 007's route in every detail should park just before the pedestrianised part of London Road – there is a convenient Asda supermarket with ample parking – and take in the pedestrian area by foot.

Bond accelerates away from Swanley Junction and hurtles around the long curve of the **Farningham bypass** at an impressive 90mph towards Wrotham Hill. Between Swanley and the village of Farningham, the course of the A20 is much changed since Bond travelled along it. The reason is the construction of the north end (junction 1) of the M20 motorway in 1971 and the M25 orbital motorway at its junction (3) with the M20 in 1986 (although a bridge built in anticipation of taking the M25 across the junction had existed since the 1970s). When Fleming was writing, there was no break in the A20 between Swanley and Farningham, but since then, the course of London Road at the southern end of Swanley has been diverted to meet the major roundabout that marks the motorway junction and the old course of the A20

Bond hurtles around this bend of the Farningham Bypass.

has been obliterated. Only when one has passed the junction, taking the fourth exit of the roundabout towards Farningham, does the original course of the A20, which the modern road follows, resume. Bond lovers who wish to avoid the maelstrom of London traffic may prefer to join 007's route at this junction.

The Farningham bypass retains the form it did when Bond flew along it, although today travelling at 90mph is not possible, not only because it breaks the speed limit, but also because a roundabout at its junction with the road to Dartford will inevitably check one's speed. From Farningham, Bond would have continued along the A20 up Gorse Hill and into the village of West Kingsdown, which in Fleming's time was known simply as Kingsdown. (To avoid confusion, Sir Hugo Drax's facilities are near the other Kingsdown, between Dover and Deal.) Just before arriving in West Kingsdown, Bond would have passed the Brands Hatch stadium. The motor racing circuit was established in 1926 and until 1950 organised motorcycling events. From the 1950s, the circuit hosted racing car events, focusing on Formula 3. In August 1950, record crowds of 46,000 saw local man George Wicken win the inaugural international challenge race (first prize: £100), beating stiff opposition from an up-and-coming driver, 20-year-old Stirling Moss. That Brands Hatch is not mentioned in *Moonraker* is odd because Fleming had an interest in motor sport. In 1932, his first foreign assignment for Reuters took him to Munich to cover the International Alpine Trials. To follow the action, he rode as navigator in driver Donald Healey's Invicta. Almost three decades later, Fleming wrote a screen treatment for an episode of an unproduced Bond television series called 'Death for Breakfast', which was set at the Nürburg circuit and featured Stirling Moss (the story was later incorporated into Anthony Horowitz's 2015 Bond novel, *Trigger Mortis*). Even in *Moonraker*, Fleming tells us that Bond once dabbled on the fringes of the motor-racing world. Presumably, Bond was driving far too fast to notice Brands Hatch on the left on his approach into West Kingsdown.

Continuing south-east on the A20 after West Kingsdown, Bond crests the top of **Wrotham Hill** and descends – probably at some speed, the hill being a 1km, 5% gradient – towards Wrotham. The current course of the A20 around Wrotham – it bypasses the village itself – and through West Malling, Larkfield and Ditton retains the course that Bond would have followed. As the A20 approaches Maidstone, at Allington, the original course has been diverted slightly to accommodate junction 5 of the M20 motorway, which did not exist in 1955. Once past the junction, drivers are back on course, with the current A20 resuming the route taken by Bond.

On London Road at Allington, 007 would have passed the Sir Thomas Wyatt inn, where Drax had stopped on his way to London just hours earlier. Bond would have continued along the A20 towards Maidstone town centre. When the A20 reaches the River Medway – London Road at this point becoming Broadway – Bond would have continued straight across the river and into the High Street. He would have continued into King Street and out of Maidstone on Ashford Road. Today, this route cannot be followed precisely. Drivers heading east are taken away from Broadway around a large roundabout and along Bishops Way, Palace Avenue, Mote Road, and Watt Tyler Way that bypasses the town centre. While it is not impossible to enter the High Street from the roundabout, the street has been partially pedestrianised, restricting access for ordinary traffic. Bond lovers may prefer to find a car park close to the town centre and explore the High Street and King Street on foot. If continuing the journey via Watt Tyler Way, head north-eastwards until you reach a large roundabout and follow signs to Bearsted, thus placing you back on to the A20. The village of Bearsted is not mentioned in *Moonraker* but given a namecheck (though erroneously located in

The long descent along Wrotham Hill, where Bond picks up speed.

Hampshire) in Fleming's non-Bond short story 'The Shameful Dream', which was written in about 1951 but not published until 2008.

Bond continues heading south-east on the A20, where, just before he passes the turning to **Leeds Castle** on his right, he achieves a speed of 95mph. From his initial journey through Kent in *Moonraker*, we know that, when he reaches the village of **Charing** where the road forks, Bond takes the left fork, which puts him on the A252 towards Canterbury. The right fork continues the A20 to Ashford. During his pursuit of Drax, after climbing Charing Hill, which he encounters immediately after again taking the left fork, Bond almost comes a cropper. Huge rolls of newspaper, which Drax's henchman, Krebs, manages to release from a lorry that had been slowing up the Mercedes, crash into the Bentley, wrecking the car and throwing Bond into a ditch. In his first run down to Drax's establishment, though, Bond continues on the A252 through the village of **Molash** and past **Chilham Castle**.

At Chilham, the road joins the A28, which leads into **Canterbury**. Details for the remainder of Bond's journey are sparse, but we know that, in

Bond passes this turning to Leeds Castle.

The Charing fork, where Bond takes the road to Canterbury.

Canterbury, Bond takes the **Old Dover Road**. This suggests that he approaches the city on Wincheap and continues into Castle Street. He turns right into Watling Street, which becomes the Old Dover Road. This connects with the Dover Road proper (the A2), taking him down to Dover. Today, the motorist can get as far as Castle Street, but is prevented by bollards from following Bond's route any further. Instead, it will be necessary, at the Wincheap roundabout, to turn right and follow the ring road along Pin Hill and Rhodaus Town, and then turn right at the next roundabout into Old Dover Road. This still joins Dover Road, but here is it redesignated the A2050. Do not join the A2 yet, but continue through the village of Bridge, whose high street preserves the original course of the A2. After Bridge, join the A2 towards Dover.

Before Bond knows it – fifteen minutes, according to Fleming's description – he is in **Dover**. The A2 would have taken Bond into the centre of Dover, but the course of the road has changed since Bond's day. About 8½km away from Dover, the original course of the road heads south-east along Lydden Hill and through the villages of Lydden, Temple Ewell and Buckland before terminating in Dover. Today, the road bypasses those villages to approach Dover from the north. It is, however, possible to come off the A2 at the junction at Lydden Hill and follow the former road course through Lydden and into Dover.

At Dover, Bond follows the road past **Dover Castle** and turns right for **Kingsdown**, stopping soon after at the World Without Want public house for a drink and to a have a chat with the innkeeper to learn more about the death of Drax's previous security officer, Major Tallon, at the hands of one of Drax's staff. Bond would have driven along Castle Hill Road out of Dover, with the castle on his right, and on to the A258 towards Deal. At Ringwould, there is a right-hand turn to Kingsdown. This route into Kingsdown can be followed today, but there is no inn called World Without Want, this being a rare invention by Fleming. There are other public houses, however, that the Bond lover may wish to stop at: the Rising Sun, the Zetland Arms, or the Kings Head. The exact location of Drax's establishment cannot

Bond would have passed the Five Bells public house before turning right towards Kingsdown.

be pinpointed – we know it is near Deal – but if one takes the coast road between Kingsdown and Walmer, one can appreciate the landscape in which it was set.

London to Ramsgate

Between them, Bond and M in *Goldfinger* hatch a plan for Bond to get close to the eponymous villain in order to discover how he is smuggling gold out of the country. With Goldfinger's centre of operations at Reculver, near Ramsgate in Kent, Bond decides to snare him with a round of golf at the Royal St Mark's course on the east coast at Sandwich (a thinly veiled Royal St George's). Taking an Aston Martin DB Mark III from the car pool to suit the adventurous, man-about-town image he wants to project to Goldfinger, Bond begins his journey from headquarters to Kent.

Fleming's description of Bond's route passes over London and commences on the **A2** on the **short hill outside Rochester**. Assuming Bond follows a similar route through London to the one he takes in *Moonraker*, he is likely to have come off the South Circular Road (A205) at Eltham to join the A2 (the old Roman road of Watling Street and known at the Eltham/A2 junction as the Rochester Way Relief Road), negotiate his way through Blackheath, and follow the A2 past Bexley, Dartford, and Gravesend and towards Rochester. Today, the A2 just west of Strood at the Three Crutches junction merges seamlessly with the M2 motorway to bypass the Medway towns. Bond lovers should stay on the A2 and continue into Strood, across Rochester Bridge over the River Medway, through the **sprawl of Rochester and Chatham**, then the **outskirts of Gillingham**, and finally Rainham before emerging from the Medway towns, staying on the A2 towards Sittingbourne.

After Sittingbourne, still on the A2, Bond observes the **endless orchards of the Faversham growers**. At the time Fleming was writing, the landscape around Sittingbourne and Faversham was known as orchard country, with large areas of orchard and plantation extending either side of the A2. The principal crop was fruit, including apples, pears, cherries, plums, and damsons, which were sold at market in Faversham and other towns or offered wholesale to fruiterers and restaurants. Bond also observes the gleam of the Thames to his left. With the Isle of Sheppey between him and the Thames Estuary, it is more likely that Bond was seeing the Swale, a channel of water separating Sheppey and the coast of Kent north of Sittingbourne and Faversham.

Immediately after Faversham, Bond turns left, coming off the A2 and heading north-east towards Whitstable on the A299. Bond derides the landscape of holiday bungalows that for him characterises the towns and villages of north-east Kent: **Whitstable, Herne Bay, Birchington and Margate**. Naturally, with its coastal views and air and open countryside, the area was popular as a place to live and visit. The bungalows that Bond dismisses so readily were relatively affordable too. In 1958, when Fleming wrote *Goldfinger*, a new bungalow, complete with central heating, built-in refrigerator, fitted kitchen, and garage, cost the princely sum of £2,170.

Continuing along the A299 past Herne Bay, Bond slows for the crossroads that signposts Reculver to the left. Bond sees the ancient monument sign for **Reculver Church** and slows, it seems, with half a mind to visit the church. The church – find it at Reculver Lane, Reculver, CT6 6SS – would not be a bad place to stop, being a picturesque ruin with gorgeous views out into the Thames Estuary. Only the imposing towers of the twelfth-century church have survived into modern times, the church being a victim of coastal erosion. Within the site of the church are the remains of a Saxon monastery that pre-dates the church, and a late Roman 'Saxon shore fort' that pre-dates the monastery. The site is in the care of English Heritage and is free to visit. Returning to the junction of the A299 with the road to Reculver (Sweechbridge Road), the ancient monument sign has been replaced by a more general brown sign with symbols pointing to the English Heritage site, a country park (where visitors to the church may park), and a camping and caravaning site.

Bond stays on the A299 after the Reculver crossroads, catches a glimpse of Goldfinger's factory on the left-hand side, probably somewhere in the vicinity of the hamlet of Potten Street, and takes a **right-hand turn across the Manston plateau to Ramsgate**. To follow in his trail, Bond lovers would need to take the third exit of the St Nicholas at Wade Roundabout to stay on the A299, and then turn left on the Monkton Roundabout to continue on the A299 (or the A253, as it was in Bond's day) towards Ramsgate.

In Ramsgate, Bond ends his journey at an inn or hotel called the Channel Packet. This appears to have been a fictional establishment, and it is difficult to identify what place, if any, Fleming had in mind, but the eighteenth-century, clifftop guesthouse, the Royal Harbour Hotel at 10 Nelson Crescent, CT11 9JF (an address that would have attracted Fleming, Nelson worshipper that he was), is a possibility and provides suitably Bondian accommodation and dining.

SOUTH-WEST

CORNWALL

Tregenna Castle Resort, Trelyon Avenue, St Ives, TR26 2DE
tregenna-castle.co.uk

The opening chapter of *On Her Majesty's Secret Service* finds Bond on the beach at Royale-les-Eaux – the fictional seaside resort in northern France that is an amalgam of Le Touquet, Dieppe, Deauville and other coastal pleasure-spots that Ian Fleming visited regularly – reminiscing about his childhood holidays at the seaside: the wet sand between the toes, the collection of shells and other beach-combed treasures, crabs in rockpools escaping the searching fingers of inquisitive children, the endless swimming and sunshine, the bucket

Porthminster Beach, St Ives, an inspiration for Bond's reminiscences in On Her Majesty's Secret Service.

and spade, the Cadbury chocolate Flake and fizzy lemonade.

Bond's trip down memory lane captures his creator's own childhood experiences. In those passages, Fleming harked back to holidays as a young child. One place the young Ian and his family holidayed was St Ives in Cornwall. The family would stay at Tregenna Castle, a grand, battlemented house built on top of a hill overlooking the harbour in 1774 and converted into a hotel – with much interior remodelling – in the late nineteenth century. A path through the hotel grounds would lead the family to Porthminster Beach, a wide stretch of sand complete with rocky outcrops that is perhaps a little more secluded than the beach at St Ives harbour.

The hotel continues to thrive, having been transformed into a resort offering holiday cottages and lodges, as well as rooms within the castle, and many facilities, including indoor and outdoor swimming pools, a gym, a golf course, tennis courts, and beauty treatments. Apart from Fleming, other luminaries of the Bond world who have stayed at the hotel include Dames Judi Dench and Joanna Lumley.

Tregenna Castle Resort, where the young Ian Fleming spent several summers.

Holywell Bay, Holywell, TR8 5PF

Holywell Bay, a beach near Newquay and popular with surfers, families, and dog walkers alike, doubled for North Korea's Pukch'ŏng coast in DIE ANOTHER DAY. Appropriately, Bond (Pierce Brosnan) infiltrates the country on a surfboard, naturally supplied by Q Branch. The waves that carry him to the shore undetected are courtesy of Hawaii, but the two rocky islets behind Bond when he steps on to the beach are Cornwall's own. These are known locally as Carter's Rocks or Gull Rocks and are a prominent landmark for visitors to Holywell Bay. The concrete border post seen in the opening moments of the film was erected on the lower part of the dunes facing the sea, approximately where the Holywell Bay Surf School is today.

If approaching Holywell Bay via Newquay, do allow plenty of time to get there. Traffic can be very slow around Newquay, especially in the height of the summer. Once at Holywell, drive through the village and, ignoring the car park next to Holywell Beach Bar, continue along Holywell Road to the National Trust Holywell Bay car park. It has ample space and is free for National Trust members.

Holywell Bay doubled for the North Korean coastline in DIE ANOTHER DAY.

The Eden Project, Bodelva Road, Bodelva, PL24 2SG
www.edenproject.com

From open-cast mine to diamond mine. The Eden Project, an ecological visitor attraction dominated by two massive dome complexes (biomes) in which rainforest and Mediterranean environments have been reconstructed, was built within a former china clay pit, opening in 2000. Two years later, the distinctive domes, built out of hexagonal, thermoplastic panels, were seen on the big screen as an Icelandic diamond mine operated by villainous

The biomes of the Eden Project were transformed into Sir Gustav Graves's lair in DIE ANOTHER DAY.

Sir Gustav Graves (Toby Stephens) in DIE ANOTHER DAY. Graves's operation is based in the rainforest biome, and behind the gantries, platforms and 'dream machine' apparatus, viewers catch glimpses of a flourishing jungle.

Visitors to the Eden Project can explore the rainforest dome without fear of being collared by henchman Mr Kil (Lawrence Makoare) or bumping into an invisible car. The visitor parking is set a little way from the visitor centre and entrance, and the biomes impressively come into view only after one has passed through the ticket desks. While it is not, of course, possible to abseil from the roof of the biome, as Jinx Johnson (Halle Berry) does in the film, there is a roof-level platform that allows visitors to look out over the rainforest canopy. Visitors looking for even greater thrills can try the giant zip wire, which runs above the Eden Project complex, including the biomes.

Incidentally, china clay from Cornwall, including the clay extracted from the Eden Project pit, was used in the manufacture of Minton china, which, as we learn in *From Russia With Love*, is Bond's favourite maker of crockery.

DEVON

North Sands Bay, Cliff Road, Salcombe, TQ8 8LD

As a boy, Ian Fleming spent three summers in a row at Salcombe, holidaying with his brothers and his mother, Evelyn. Salcombe is a picturesque fishing town on the mouth of the Kingsbridge estuary on the south-west coast of England and is well worth a visit in any case, but the literary connection – the town, like

***Ian Fleming may have remembered the beaches of Salcombe when he began to write* On Her Majesty's Secret Service.**

St Ives in Cornwall, may have inspired Bond's childhood memories described at the beginning of *On Her Majesty's Secret Service* – provides an extra incentive to any Bond lover. The town is characterised by narrow, hilly streets of brightly painted Victorian houses and tourist shops that look out to the boats moored in the harbour. Art galleries and high-street fashion boutiques compete with fish and chip restaurants, ice cream parlours, and shops selling the accoutrements of a fun day at the beach.

Salcombe has several beaches, which are situated on the east and west sides of the estuary. North Sands, located to the south of the town on the west side of the harbour, matches the description in the novel, with its soft sand, seaweed-fringed rockpools, and fine swimming, but it may be that Fleming and his family sought something more secluded.

WILTSHIRE

Warneford Place, Sevenhampton, Swindon, SN6 7QA

Ian and Ann Fleming moved into what would be Ian's final house, Sevenhampton Place in the village of Sevenhampton near Swindon, in June 1963. It was Ann's ideal home, but it was far from in an ideal state when the Flemings bought the house in 1959. It required considerable repair, renovation and refurbishment, and it was four years before the couple could take up residence. The relocation took Ian away from his beloved Kent coast, but he consoled himself with the fact that he was reasonably close to Huntercombe golf club and his old haunts in Nettlebed.

As with Bekesbourne before it, Sevenhampton Place is a substantial mansion set with a secluded landscape of fields and woodland and water features. In a letter to Evelyn Waugh, Ann Fleming described its forty bedrooms, billiard room and ballroom, though these rooms would be considerably altered. Ian Fleming never warmed to the house like he had his others, complaining to Amherst Villiers, who is credited in *Moonraker* for supercharging Bond's 4½-litre Bentley, that he spent his time cutting down nettles and scraping mushrooms off his clothes because of the lake.

Today, Sevenhampton Place, now known as Warneford Place, is inaccessible to the public, but Highworth Road, the main road through the village, passes the gateway and driveway that leads to the house, and the south-east side of St James's Church overlooks the estate. Roves Lane, which extends south from Highworth Road, runs down the west side of the estate.

St James's Church, Rove Lane, Sevenhampton, Swindon, SN6 7QA

Ian Fleming died on 12 August 1964, not in Wiltshire, but in Kent, where he had travelled to be elected captain of the Royal St George's golf club in Sandwich. He is buried, however, at Sevenhampton, and his grave and monument can be seen in the churchyard of St James's Church.

The grave is in fact a family tomb, being the resting place not only of Ian, but of Ann, and their son Caspar. The plaque dedicated to Ann, who died in 1981, offers the inscription, 'There is none like her, none', a line taken from Maud (Part XVIII), a poem by Alfred, Lord Tennyson. The epitaph to Caspar, who died tragically young in 1975, reads, 'To cease upon the midnight with no pain', which is a quotation from Keats's 'Ode to a Nightingale'. The plaque dedicated to Ian Fleming is different in several ways. It does not give his full name (Ann's and Caspar's middle names are provided), it gives the full dates of his birth and death (the other plaques record only the years of birth and death), and in addition to the epitaph, includes the words, 'In Memoriam', which the others lack.

Ian Fleming's epitaph has a classical source. It reads, 'Omnia perfunctus vitae praemia, marces', and is taken from *On the Nature of Things* (*De rerum natura*), a six-book didactic poem written in honour of the Greek philosopher Epicurus by the Roman writer Lucretius, who lived during the first half of the first century BC. The phrase derives from book three, lines 355 to 362, which in part explores the fear of death, and can be translated as, 'All the rewards of a fulfilled life now decay'. On their own, the words refer to the inevitability of death and the impermanence of life and material things, but also allude to Fleming's intense, somewhat hedonistic, take on life. The phrase also echoes James Bond's philosophy, as revealed in the novel of *You Only Live Twice* and recalled at the end of NO TIME TO DIE: 'The proper function of man is to live. I shall not waste my days in trying to prolong them. I shall use my days.' These words, incidentally, were not original to Fleming, but attributed to American writer Jack London.

Within its original passage, the line on Fleming's plaque has a rather more sinister connotation: 'Put away your tears, buffoon, and cease the complaints. All the rewards of a fulfilled life now decay. But because you always reach for that which is absent, life, imperfect and disagreeable, slips away from you, and death stops at your head before you are satisfied and full.'

The passage clearly concerns premature death and from its Epicurean viewpoint ridicules the notion that the pursuit of pleasure leads to fulfilment. While happiness, according to Epicurus, derives from the absence of suffering, overindulgence can be a cause of pain, and ultimately unhappiness and death. For anyone who knows their classics, the words that follow those selected for Fleming offer something of a scorpion-like sting in the tail; he died prematurely aged just 56 of a heart attack following years of heavy smoking and drinking.

The obelisk at St James's Church, Sevenhampton, that marks the grave of Ian Fleming.

EAST

CAMBRIDGESHIRE

Orton Mere Station, Orton Mere, Peterborough, PE2 7DL
www.nvr.org.uk

The Nene Valley Railway, a heritage railway between Peterborough and Yarwell that preserves stations along the line and maintains and runs vintage trains, was used extensively for the filming of the thrilling railway-based scenes in OCTOPUSSY. During 1982, filming took place on the stretch of line between Orton Mere and Wansford, with stations and buildings along the track being transformed, with the help of set dressing and the use of military vehicles and Continental rolling stock, into the railway system of Soviet-era East Germany.

Bond passes through Orton Mere Station in an unconventional locomotive in OCTOPUSSY.

Orton Mere station, the first stop after Peterborough, is seen briefly in the film. Bond (Roger Moore) has jumped into General Orlov's (Steven Berkoff) black Mercedes and is pursuing a train taking Octopussy (Maud Adams), her travelling circus, and a nuclear bomb into West Germany. With the car's tyres having been shot off, Bond manoeuvres the car on to the tracks and is directly behind the train. As the train approaches a station, a signalman in a signal box sees the car and quickly changes the points, diverting the car on to a parallel track. The train and the car pass through the station together, much to the surprise of passengers waiting on the platform.

The station is in reality Orton Mere, which is located on a lane, also called Orton Mere, off the A605. There is a car park at the end of the lane, and the station is a few hundred metres beyond that. As one approaches the station, one passes the signal box that put Bond on a different track.

Overton Station (for Ferry Meadows), Orton Wistow, Peterborough, PE2 5UU
www.nvr.org.uk

The dramatic scene in OCTOPUSSY in which General Orlov, having been shot in the back by East German border guards, crawls along the tracks in a vain attempt to catch the train taking Octopussy's circus and a nuclear bomb into West Germany, was filmed at Overton Station (formerly Ferry Meadows Station) on the Nene Valley Railway. Several parts of the station complex can be seen in the sequence. Before crossing into West Germany, Octopussy's train stops at the border station for inspection, giving audiences a view of Overton's platform and station building. Orlov arrives in a black Mercedes, which speeds over Overton's level crossing on Ham Lane and into the railway yard opposite the station platform. At the same time, a Soviet army helicopter carrying General Gogol (Walter Gotell) lands in the yard. The West German border was located east of the platform, a short way down the track.

Remarkably, Overton Station made a second appearance in a James Bond film. In GOLDENEYE, an armoured train carrying villains Alec Trevelyan (Sean Bean), Xenia Onatopp (Famke Janssen), and Colonel Ourumov (Gottfried John), as well as kidnapped computer programmer Natalya Simonova (Izabella Scorupco), passes through a Russian station, having left St Petersburg. The station building at Overton was heavily disguised for the scene to make it look more Russian, but the station platform can clearly be seen. The Russian railway workers in the foreground were positioned on the edge of the railway yard.

Today, there is little trace of the Cold War infrastructure represented in either film at Overton Station, the temporary

Overton Station featured in ***OCTOPUSSY*** *and* ***GOLDENEYE.***

border crossing towers, fences and station cladding having been removed on completion of filming, and it is no easy task to relate the station as it appears now to how it is seen in the films. A canopy added to the station building since the filming of the GOLDENEYE scene alters the building's appearance still further, although it is very pleasant to sit under, and it delightfully evokes the heyday of the Great Northern Railway.

The station, like all stations on the Nene Valley Railway, is free to visit, but do spend money in the station's café or second-hand bookshop; all proceeds go to the upkeep of the station. If travelling to Overton by car, then park in the car park of the Ferry Meadows County Park on Ham Lane – a small fee is payable – and take a five-minute walk to Overton station from there. After your visit, rather than returning immediately to your vehicle, I recommend taking the train from Overton to the next Bond-related stop on the line, Wansford Station. Apart from providing an opportunity to ride in a vintage train that will undoubtedly recall, among other railway scenes from the film series, Bond's (Sean Connery) encounter with Grant (Robert Shaw) on the Orient Express in FROM RUSSIA WITH LOVE, the journey allows the Bond lover to travel along the line that appears in the scenes between stations in OCTOPUSSY and GOLDENEYE.

Wansford Station, Old Great North Road, Stibbington, Peterborough, PE8 6LR
www.nvr.org.uk

Several key scenes in OCTOPUSSY were filmed at Wansford Station, the penultimate station on the Nene Valley Railway when travelling west from Peterborough to Yarwell. The sequence where General Orlov (Steven Berkoff) meets Kamal Khan (Louis Jourdan) at Karl Marx Stadt station to supervise the loading of a nuclear bomb into one of the carriages of the train that will take Octopussy's circus into West Germany was filmed at the west end of the former main station building on the north platform and in the yard to the front (that is, the north side) of the building. On the south side of the building, there is much activity, as circus performers and staff, including Octopussy's (Maud Adams) lieutenant Magda (Kristina Wayborn), board the train at the platform. We also see Bond (Roger Moore) among the crowd, carrying a large basket to blend in as he attempts to discover what Kamal Khan and General Orlov are up to.

In a later scene, Bond steals a black Mercedes belonging to General Orlov's staff and speeds off in pursuit of the train, steering the car through a level crossing and on to the tracks. The level crossing is on the Old Great North Road between the present main station building and railway cottages

Wansford Station, where circus equipment and a nuclear bomb were loaded on to a train.

(nos 6, 10, 12, 18 and 20) immediately to the north. A signal box at the east end of the crossing opposite Railway Cottages can clearly be seen in the sequence. The film returns to Wansford Station when Bond's Mercedes, having been switched to a different track, collides with an oncoming train, and is catapulted over a railway viaduct and into a river, where people are fishing. The bridge, which spans the River Nene itself, is a few metres to the east of the level crossing.

There is much for the Bond lover to see and do at Wansford Station, with many of the buildings and structures present today being recognisable from the film. If arriving by car, park in a small, free parking area on Old Great North Road opposite the present main station building and next to the level crossing. (Before entering the station, and for the perfect view of the river and viaduct, walk through the small gate at the parking area and down some steps to the river edge.) As you

The level crossing seen in Octopussy, where Bond joins the tracks in General Orlov's Mercedes.

wander around the station platforms, note the red-painted carriage with black roof on the south platform underneath a footbridge. This is a preserved carriage from the train of Octopussy's circus (number 231-8-17, for the railway buffs among you). Stop on top of the footbridge for great views of the station complex, including the former station building (built in 1846) and the yard beyond it to the north. The yard is currently not accessible to visitors, but one can of course walk along the platform beside the building (large basket optional). If arriving at the station in style in a vintage train from Peterborough, the train will pull up along this platform.

Another scene in the film, a gunfight between Bond and Soviet soldiers at the entrance to a tunnel, was filmed at Wansford Tunnel, approximately 500m west of Wansford Station. Naturally, the tunnel is not accessible to visitors, but a public footpath between the villages of Sibson (next to Wansford Station) and Yarwell takes walkers to the top of the cutting at the west (Yarwell) end of the tunnel. Use Ordnance Survey Explorer Map 227 to follow the route.

BEDFORDSHIRE

Luton Hoo Hotel, The Mansion House, Luton, LU1 3TQ

www.lutonhoo.co.uk

In 1983, James Bond fans were treated to the release of two Bond films. One was OCTOPUSSY, starring Roger Moore and made by EON Productions; the other was NEVER SAY NEVER AGAIN, which saw Sean Connery back in the dinner suit. The latter was essentially a remake of THUNDERBALL and produced by film-maker Kevin McClory, who had co-written screen treatments on which Ian Fleming's novel of *Thunderball* was based and retained rights to the story.

Naturally, THUNDERBALL and NEVER SAY NEVER AGAIN had much in common, including a spell for Bond in the Shrublands health farm. In the 1983 film, the Shrublands scenes were shot just outside Luton at Luton Hoo, a late eighteenth-century mansion built in the neo-classical style by Robert Adam for the third Earl of Bute and set in extensive grounds landscaped by Capability Brown. On screen, Bond drives up to the front of the house and enters via its magnificent portico, built in the manner of a Greek temple, with ionic columns supporting the entablature and pediment. The film also made use of some of the staircases and reception areas inside the house.

Bond returned to Luton Hoo, this time for EON Productions, in THE WORLD IS NOT ENOUGH. The scene in which Bond (Pierce Brosnan) is obliged to wait at the bottom of a spiral staircase at the Baku residence of Elecktra King (Sophie Marceau) made use of the glorious grand staircase in the Mansion House.

Luton Hoo appeared as Shrublands health farm in NEVER SAY NEVER AGAIN.

Luton Hoo is today a luxurious hotel complex, with prices to match. A weekend break there will be a rare treat for many Bond lovers, but it is highly recommended, not least as it provides an opportunity to recreate several Bondian experiences. Like Bond, one can pull up to the main entrance and enter via the classical-style portico, or sit in a chair at the foot of the grand staircase. A session in the spa will give visitors a taste of Shrublands, and on the golf course one can pretend to pit one's wits against Goldfinger. Do book a table at Adam's Brasserie – one of two restaurants at the hotel – where photographs of films that were shot at Luton Hoo, including both Bond films, adorn the walls. Also of interest is the Fabergé Suite, which once housed the Fabergé collection, including bejewelled Easter eggs, of Sir Julius Wernher, who owned Luton Hoo from 1903. His art collection is now in the care of English Heritage and can be seen at Ranger's House (SE10 8QX) in Greenwich Park.

ESSEX

The Storehouse, The Quay, Wivenhoe, Colchester, CO7 9BX

Richard Chopping's style of artwork that adorns the cover of the Jonathan Cape edition of *From Russia With Love*, with its distinctive trompe-l'œil elements on wood grain, rapidly became an essential part of the iconography of the literary Bond. After *From Russia With Love*, Ian Fleming commissioned Chopping for the cover of every Bond book from *Goldfinger* to *You Only Live Twice*. Cape stuck with Chopping for Fleming's *Octopussy and the Living Daylights*, published posthumously,

and returned to him for the cover of John Gardner's first Bond novel, *Licence Renewed*, published in 1981.

The covers for the Bond books were painted at Chopping's studio at the Storehouse, a house on the quay of the fishing village of Wivenhoe on the River Colne that he bought with his partner and fellow artist Denis Wirth-Miller in 1944 (although they did not move in until 1948). The house combined a townhouse dating to around 1800 and a

The Storehouse, Wivenhoe, where Richard Chopping painted his iconic covers for the Bond novels.

fishermen's storage building that both needed much renovation. Amazingly, the building survived the North Sea Flood of 1953 and a house fire in 1963, and still stands today. The Store House (rather than Storehouse) is a private residence, but the front of the house can be seen from the very picturesque quayside. Parking on the quay is very limited, but a free car park is situated about five minutes' walk away on Clifton Terrace.

Tiptree Tea Room, Museum and Jam Shop, Factory Hill, Tiptree, Colchester, CO5 0RF
www.tiptree.com

While at home between missions, Bond's typical breakfast, as we learn in *From Russia With Love*, comprises a single boiled egg, coffee, toast, strawberry jam, and marmalade, all served on Minton china. The jam, produced by Wilkin and Sons Ltd, is Tiptree's Little Scarlet, and it is still made today and available from the larger supermarkets. Alternatively, a supply of the preserve may be bought at the shop within the farm and factory complex, which remains to this day in Tiptree, south-west of Colchester. Combine a trip to the shop with a tour of the farm, a visit

The Tiptree jam factory, makers of James Bond's favourite conserve.

to the museum, and refreshments at the tea room for a very good day out. The tea room aims to provide Little Scarlet with its cream teas, but be aware that the provision of the jam depends on the harvest and is not guaranteed.

NORFOLK

Creake Abbey ruins, Creake Road, Fakenham, NR21 9LF

In May 1953, a letter purporting to be from James Bond but in fact written by Ian Fleming was published in the *Sunday Times* and asked whether some of the treasure that supposedly lay buried in England could not be located using mining and salvage prospecting methods. The letter reflected Fleming's long-held fascination with treasure hunting, as evident from the plot of *Live and Let Die*, involving as it does the recovery by Mr Big of a hoard of seventeenth-century gold coins to provide funds for Soviet spy organisation Smersh. Through the letter, Fleming sought readers' suggestions for 'well-substantiated' stories of buried treasure. He would choose one and, with the paper's financial backing, investigate it.

Fleming settled on Creake Abbey in Norfolk, which he chose because of its spectral name and its location only a mile south of Admiral Nelson's birthplace at Burnham Thorpe.

Tales of treasure at the abbey date back at least to the early sixteenth century, when a defrocked Benedictine monk named William Stapleton attempted to locate the treasure with the help of the spirits of deceased monks. Fleming was better equipped. He enlisted a team from the Royal Engineers, who wanted to test their new metal-detecting equipment, which had been developed to locate unexploded bombs, a legacy of the Second World War. The Sappers brought a bomb locator and a Polish mine detector, which had different detecting capabilities. The survey proceeded systematically, covering the floor of the abbey church, the cloister, the cloister garth or ornamental garden, the site of the chapter house and the abbot's lodging. The machines were run in planned walks up and down the survey area; when the operators obtained a 'fix', a label was planted ready for the spot to be dug.

So, what did they find? Thirty nails, one frying pan, one mole trap, one oil drum, sardine tins and 'about a hundredweight' of scrap iron. Nothing was thought to be earlier than the late nineteenth century, and most belonged to the twentieth. Nevertheless, Fleming was satisfied with his work, and without realising it he became a pioneer of archaeological metal detecting. Just a handful of systematic surveys had been carried out by 1953, and it was only after the late 1960s that metal detecting became a regular part of archaeological prospecting.

The abbey ruins are in the care of English Heritage and can be visited free of charge by the public all year round.

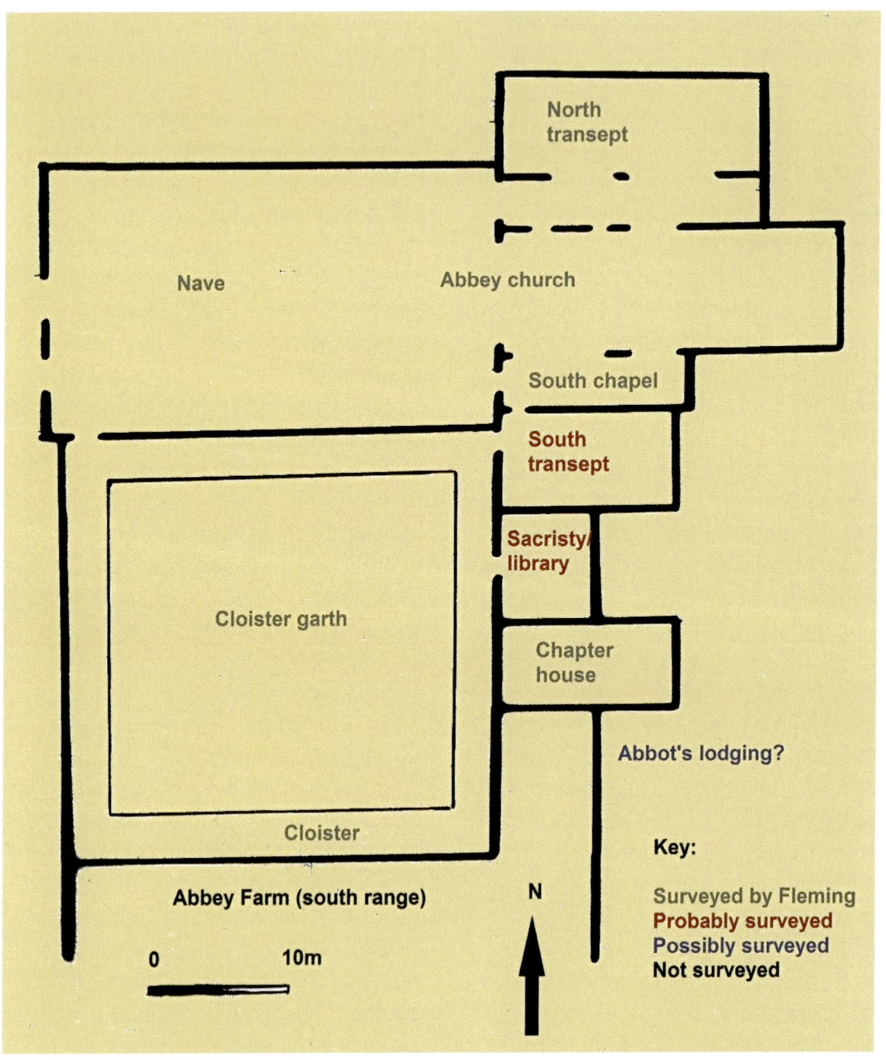

A plan of Creake Abbey, showing where Ian Fleming conducted his pioneering metal-detecting survey.

7

MIDLANDS AND NORTH

CHESHIRE

41 Liverpool Road, Chester, CH2 1AB
Daniel Craig, whose tenure as Bond ran for five films from 2006 to 2021, was born at his parents' home in Liverpool Road in Chester in 1968. The semi-detached house is situated at the southern end of the road, opposite Victoria Crescent and on the corner of Liverpool Road and Rock Lane.

Liverpool Road, Chester, where Daniel Craig was born. (Photo by Rob Glew)

DERBYSHIRE

Strutts Centre, Derby Road, Belper, DE56 1UU

Timothy Dalton, who took the role of Bond in two films, THE LIVING DAYLIGHTS and LICENCE TO KILL, was born in 1946 in Colwyn Bay in North Wales, but he grew up in the north of England, his family moving to Belper in Derbyshire when he was aged 4. As a teenager, he attended the Herbert Strutt School, known locally as 'Strutts', a grammar school that was built in the Jacobean style in 1908, opened the following year, and named after a local alderman who funded its construction. The site continues today as a community centre.

GREATER MANCHESTER

The Robert Shaw, 34–40 Market Street, Westhoughton, Bolton, BL5 3AN

Robert Shaw, who memorably played SPECTRE agent 'Red' Grant in FROM RUSSIA WITH LOVE, was born in Westhoughton in 1927. His connection with the town has been commemorated with a blue plaque at the town hall and the naming after him of a Wetherspoons public house. Inside

Strutts Community Centre, Derby Road. (Photo by Alan Murray-Rust, CC BY-SA 2.0 https://creativecommons.org/licenses/by-sa/2.0, via Wikimedia Commons)

the pub, there is a set of photographs of the actor, accompanied by a brief biography, which curiously omits to mention his role in the Bond film.

LANCASHIRE

Morecambe Heritage, Unit 29 Arndale Centre, Market Street, LA4 5DH
morecambleheritage.co.uk

Morecambe Bay is familiar to James Bond lovers as the place that Ruby Windsor, one of Blofeld's 'angels of death', hails from, as revealed in *On Her Majesty's Secret Service*. In the film version, Ruby Windsor becomes Ruby Bartlett (Angela Scoular), but her hometown is unchanged. In both book and film, Ruby comes from a family of poultry farmers, and it was the experience of working on the farm that resulted in her developing an allergy to chickens, something that Blofeld is keen to cure.

Ian Fleming did his research. A visit to the archive of the *Morecambe Guardian* and a trawl through its classified columns confirms that there were many poultry farms in the Morecambe region at the time Fleming was writing in the early 1960s. There was a concentration of farms in the Carnforth area further around the bay to the north-east of Morecambe, another on Oxcliffe Road on the southern edge of Morecambe, and several farms a little way inland near Halton or Caton on the River Lune.

If visiting or holidaying in Morecambe, explore the countryside where the poultry farms once existed, then drop into Morecambe Heritage, which tells the story of the town in bygone days. Look out for artefacts, documents, and photographs dating between the late 1940s and 1960s, which illustrate the environment in which Ruby Windsor or Bartlett would have been raised.

YORKSHIRE

National Science and Media Museum, Pictureville, Bradford, BD1 1NQ
www.scienceandmediamuseum.org.uk

Following a £16 million refurbishment, the National Museum of Photography, Film and Television in Bradford – now the National Science and Media Museum – was reopened on 16 June 1999 by the then James Bond, Pierce Brosnan. Huge crowds gathered to catch a glimpse of the actor, whose latest Bond film, THE WORLD IS NOT ENOUGH, was just months away. The ceremony had special resonance for Brosnan.
A new, 106-seat, cinema formed part of the revamp and extension, and this was named in honour of one of the original, legendary producers of the Bond films. The Cubby Broccoli Cinema plays an integral part of the museum's film and event calendar. Over the years, it has hosted film festivals, special showings, and lectures, and trialled innovative

The National Science and Media Museum. (Photo by Chemical Engineer, CC BY-SA 4.0 https://creativecommons.org/licenses/by-sa/4.0, via Wikimedia Commons)

cinematic and broadcast technologies. Situated in the city centre, the museum is well served by public transport and easily reached by car.

Royal Armouries Museum, Armouries Drive, Leeds, LS10 1LT
royalarmouries.org

Mention the words Walther PPK to anyone and the chances are they will identify it as James Bond's gun of choice. There cannot be many fictional characters whose handguns are so deeply embedded in popular culture. Dirty Harry's .44 Magnum is one of the few other examples. The Walther PPK is so closely associated with Bond that any description or history of the weapon is likely to allude to its most famous user. The Royal Armouries in Leeds, which contains a permanent display of guns that feature in the Bond novels, is a case in point. On display there is naturally a Walther PPK, which featured in the novels after *Dr No* and in most of the films, and a Beretta 1919/318, which Bond uses until the events of *Dr No*, and these are joined by a host of other weapons mentioned in the books, among them a Luger Model 1908, Sauer Model 38-H,

The Royal Armouries Museum, Leeds. (Photo by Jeff Buck, CC BY-SA 2.0 https://creativecommons.org/licenses/by-sa/2.0, via Wikimedia Commons)

a Colt Hammerless Pocket Model, and a Smith & Wesson Airweight Model 12. If you want to learn more about Bond's weapons, then a trip to the Royal Armouries is well worthwhile.

The Wensleydale Heifer, Main Street, West Whitton, Leyburn, DL8 4LS
www.wensleydaleheifer.co.uk

One of the attractions of this five-star hotel and restaurant in the heart of the Yorkshire Dales is its themed bedrooms. Curiously enough, there are two James-themed rooms. One is dedicated to Yorkshire vet and writer James Herriot of *All Creatures Great and Small* fame, the other to James Bond. Exuding luxury and decorated with Bond-style furnishings, the latter is sure to delight any Bond fan.

WARWICKSHIRE

British Motor Museum, Banbury Road, Gaydon, CV35 0BJ
www.britishmotormuseum.co.uk

Have you noticed how everyone in the Daniel Craig era of James Bond films tends to drive vehicles manufactured by Jaguar Land Rover? It seems that all organisations, even villainous ones, like to benefit from company car arrangements. In SKYFALL, for example, Bond begins a pursuit of an assassin in Turkey in a Land Rover Defender 110 driven by Moneypenny (Naomie Harris). In SPECTRE, Spectre's henchmen negotiate the snow-covered mountain slopes of Austria in a Range Rover Sport SVR and a couple of Land Rover Defender 'Bigfoot' vehicles. In NO TIME TO DIE, Bond and Madeleine Swann (Léa Seydoux) are chased through a Norwegian forest by Safin's (Rami Malek) goons in another Land Rover Defender. Some of these vehicles, including the Defender used in SKYFALL, and models like those that appear in the films, are on display at the British Motor Museum, which celebrates the heritage of the British motor industry, particularly in the Midlands. Look for the vehicles on display in the museum's 'Film and TV cars' section.

8

WALES

Blaen-y-pant House, 76 Blaen-Y-Pant Crescent, Newport, NP20 5PX

Blaen-y-pant House was the childhood home of Desmond Llewelyn, his parents moving there not long after his birth in Newport on 12 September 1914. The actor was best known for playing gadget-master Q in all the Bond films between 1963 and 1999, except LIVE AND LET DIE in 1973. He also made a brief appearance in CHITTY CHITTY BANG BANG. Ben Whishaw, who played Q during Daniel Craig's tenure as Bond, noted in an interview with Graham Norton that there is great public affection for the character of Q, helped in no small part by Llewelyn's portrayal and the public's familiarity and

Blaen-y-pant House, the birthplace of Desmond Llewelyn. (Photo by Joyce Compton)

enjoyment of the Q–Bond interplay and exchanges in the films. When the film-makers developed the role of Q, they could not have foreseen how successful the character would become, even away from Bond. The characters of Benji Dunn in the MISSION: IMPOSSIBLE films and Lucius Fox in Christopher Nolan's BATMAN films both owe something to the character of Q. Today MI6 has a technology development section run by officers who are all known as Q. None of this would have happened without Desmond Llewelyn's character-defining portrayal.

Today, the place where Llewelyn grew up is a care home run by Newport City Council. Access is understandably restricted, but good views of the house may be gained from the busy main road (A4042) that runs past it. The house is situated on a hill – its name means 'top of the hollow' – overlooking the Malpas Brook and Monmouthshire Canal. During Llewelyn's childhood, before the road became a dual carriageway and the treeline had increased in height, the setting would have been quite rural and the prospect across the valley spectacular.

57 Kingsland Terrace, Pontypridd, CF37 1RX

In an interview with Mark Edlitz, Don Black, the legendary lyricist responsible for the words to many a Bond theme, was unequivocal: the theme for THUNDERBALL is about James Bond. Yet, to my mind, the lyrics seem to suit Largo, the villain of the film, or indeed any archetypal Bond villain, much better. It is a neat lyrical trick and perhaps serves to underscore that hero and villain, as Scaramanga once observed, may not be so very different. That the song has such impact is down not just to Black's wordsmithing, or John Barry's rousing music, but the song's powerful delivery by Tom Jones, one of the few singers who could follow fellow Welsh native Shirley Bassey after her GOLDFINGER triumph.

Jones, originally Woodward, was born in 1940 in the front room of his grandmother's house in Kingsland Terrace in Treforest, a suburb of Pontypridd. But for a few superficial changes, from the outside, the unassuming houses appear to be largely as they looked over eighty years' ago, and there is no sign of the street's link with one of the world's biggest singing superstars.

New Theatre, Park Place, Cardiff, CF10 3LN

It was three films into the James Bond series before the theme song was used as the accompaniment to the opening titles and the musical break between the pre-title sequence and the start of the film proper. The original theme song, Monty Norman's James Bond theme, is played straight after the opening gun barrel in DR NO, while Matt Monro is heard crooning 'From Russia With Love' at the end of the film of the

Some of Dame Shirley Bassey's earliest performances were at Cardiff's New Theatre.

same name. The film-makers may not have recognised necessarily that they had found the ideal placement with the use of Shirley Bassey's bombastic 'Goldfinger' over the opening titles of GOLDFINGER, but the placement stuck, and the formula was set. Since then, many theme songs, notably Tom Jones's 'Thunderball', k.d. lang's 'Surrender' (played over the end credits of TOMORROW NEVER DIES), and Adele's 'Skyfall', have attempted to recapture the Shirley Bassey factor.

The producers could not have chosen a better singer to catapult audiences into Bond's third adventure. From the first moment Bassey performed professionally, showbusiness insiders and reporters recognised that she was heading for fame and fortune. One of Bassey's earliest performances was at the New Theatre in her home city of Cardiff. There, in March 1954, aged 17, she sang in the touring revue *Hot From Harlem*. As she toured the UK with this and other shows, press notices were entirely positive, declaring her 'a sensational songstress', 'a pleasing singer', 'an exciting new singing star', and 'a singer with real zip'. Somewhat presciently, *Picturegoer* magazine asked in 1955: 'Why don't they [British filmdom] sign up a ... young woman from Cardiff named Shirley Bassey? Shirley has oomph, come-hither or "it' – call that certain something what you will.' The question was answered nine years later when John Barry, who wrote the GOLDFINGER score, gave Bassey the chance to belt out his theme song (co-written by Leslie Bricusse and Anthony Newley).

The cityscape of Bassey's childhood – she was born on Bute Street in the Tiger Bay area of Cardiff in 1937 and grew up in the nearby suburb of Splott – has changed enormously over eighty-odd years, and the buildings associated with her have gone, but it is still possible to visit the New Theatre in Park Place that helped put her on the road to stardom.

Ty Gwyn, 32 Fairwater Road, Cardiff, CF5 2LE

At the entrance to the drive of Ty Gwyn, there is a blue plaque marking the birthplace, on 13 September 1916, of Roald Dahl, Royal Air Force pilot, intelligence officer, children's author, screenwriter of two of Ian Fleming's works – YOU ONLY LIVE TWICE and CHITTY CHITTY BANG BANG – and friend of Fleming himself.

Dahl's friendship with Fleming began in the Second World War. In spring 1942, the 25-year-old pilot Roald Dahl arrived at the British Embassy in Washington DC to serve as Assistant Air Attaché. His mission in Washington was, ostensibly, to liaise with officials of Allied air forces and represent the interests of the RAF. In reality, Dahl was recruited into the British Security Coordination, a body devoted to intelligence gathering, counter-espionage and special operations in the US. It was while serving in this capacity that Dahl came into Fleming's orbit. Dahl and Fleming formed a close friendship, and the two would meet socially, as well as professionally, during Ian's visits to New York and Washington.

After the war, Dahl lived in New York as a jobbing writer and collector of art on behalf of Charles Marsh, a philanthropist who, incidentally, was one of Fleming's near neighbours in Jamaica. Dahl and Fleming continued to meet in New York, and it was there in 1951 or 1952, during a dinner party hosted by a mutual friend, that Fleming gave Dahl an idea for a story that would become one of Roald's most celebrated pieces of adult writing. 'Lamb to the Slaughter', in which Mary kills her husband with a frozen leg of lamb, then cooks the meat and serves it to the investigating policemen, thus destroying the murder weapon, was published in America by Alfred Knopf in 1953 in *Someone Like You*, Roald's second collection of short stories.

Dahl did not often have good things to say about his fellow authors, but for Fleming he had nothing but praise. He thought the Bond author a better writer than he (Fleming) gave himself credit for, and described his company as sparky, witty, caustic and never dull.

Roald Dahl Plass, Cardiff Bay, Cardiff, CF10 5AL

The Oval Basin in Cardiff Bay was renamed Roald Dahl Plass in honour of the Cardiff-born writer in 2003. The amphitheatre-style open-air venue hosts concerts and other events and, with its views of the bay and its many shops and eateries, is an excellent area to explore.

Roald Dahl Plass, Cardiff Bay.

SCOTLAND

Eilean Donan Castle, Dornie, Kyle of Lochalsh, Highland, IV40 8DX
www.eileandonancastle.com

Following the funeral of Sir Robert King (David Calder) at his Scottish estate in THE WORLD IS NOT ENOUGH, the MI6 operation moves to its Scottish headquarters, a remote castle on a loch. There we learn more about Renard (Robert Carlyle), the mysterious terrorist behind the plot that involved King's assassination, bid farewell to Q (Desmond Llewelyn), and discover how Bond (Pierce Brosnan), injured on the roof of the O2 arena, manages to get himself passed fit for active duty with the help of Dr Molly Warmflash (Serena Scott Thomas).

The sequence was filmed at Eilean Donan Castle, a location that is no stranger to the big screen; Sean Connery fans will recognise the castle as a key location in the 1986 time-busting, sword-clashing epic HIGHLANDER. The castle, which has thirteenth-century origins, is open to the public and is an essential stop on any visit to the region.

Glencoe Mountain Resort, White Corries, Ballachulish, Highland, PH49 4HZ
www.glencoemountain.co.uk

From a conversation at the College of Arms in *On Her Majesty's Secret Service* and M's obituary for Bond in *You Only Live Twice*, we learn that James's father, Andrew, was from Glencoe or, rather, a village very near it, and that he, along with his wife, Monique Delacroix, was a keen mountaineer. Glencoe sits at the mouth of the River Coe at the north-western end of Glen Coe on the southern shore of Loch Leven. It is an excellent base for exploring the region, striking out on highland hikes, and getting active on the loch. However, to experience something of Andrew Bond's world, then a visit to the Glencoe Mountain Resort is a must. There, you may take a chairlift up the Meall a'Bhùiridh mountain to either or both of its two viewpoints – the highest of which sits at 2,200ft (670m) – for fantastic views, cloud permitting, of the mountain range. Depending on the season, you can walk, ski or bike down the mountain. There is a café at the

The Glencoe Mountain Resort, a good base to explore the landscape in which Andrew Bond, Bond's father, grew up.

resort centre, and there are camping facilities for anyone wishing to prolong their stay.

Glen Etive Road, Highland, PH49 4JA

Having almost reached his family home, Skyfall, in the film of the same name, Bond (Daniel Craig) makes a stop by a river in a mist-soaked Scottish glen for a moment of contemplation. He is joined by M (Judi Dench) and the two briefly discuss Bond's origins under ominous clouds. The scene connects the cinematic and literary Bonds, confirming that both grew up in the Highlands and were orphaned. The scene, which has become every bit as iconic as the views of Sean Connery's Bond in Switzerland's Furka Pass in GOLDFINGER that inspired it, right down to the same Aston Martin DB5, was filmed on the Glen Etive road, a winding, narrow road that runs beside the River Etive between impressive mountain ranges. The precise location shown in SKYFALL has become such an attraction that it is pinpointed on Google Maps, but for the record, it can be found on Ordnance Survey mapping (Explorer map 384 is ideal) at National Grid Reference NN202513. The spot is best reached from the A82 trunk road;

the turning into the Glen Etive road is about 2½km north-west of the Glencoe Mountain Resort.

You will need to drive along the road cautiously; it is single track and there will almost certainly be hikers, sightseers, and wild campers on the verges. For oncoming traffic and any vehicles behind you eager to overtake, there are frequent passing places to duck into. Keep an eye on where the next passing place is located; there is no shame in pulling into one earlier than may be necessary. If you and an oncoming vehicle meet between passing places, then it will mean an awkward reversing manoeuvre for one of you.

There is no parking at the SKYFALL location. While you could stop at the passing place closest to the spot, it is not ideal; not only is parking there not permitted, but a snatched selfie or rapid recreation of the filmed sequence do not do justice to the scene or scenery. There are occasional areas of reasonably flat ground off the road that provide space for a car or two, and, if you are prepared for a 4½km walk back along the road to the SKYFALL spot, there is a proper parking area a short distance west of

The Glen Etive road has seen many more visitors since the release of SKYFALL.

Dalness Lodge (postcode: PH49 4JA), a house, incidentally, that is not entirely un-Skyfall-like in appearance. Use the car park to turn round and return to the A82.

A82, Highland, PH49 4HZ

For part of their journey through Scotland to Bond's ancestral home at Skyfall in the film of the same name, 007 (Daniel Craig) and M (Judi Dench) drive along a stretch of arrow-straight road between awesome mountain slopes (the Meall a'Bhùiridh massif on the left and Beinn a'Chrùlaiste on the right). They are heading north – actually north-west – on the A82 towards Glencoe, this stretch of road being located between a viewpoint overlooking Loch Tulla to the south and the turning for the Glencoe Mountain Resort to the north. The A82 is a busy road, and stopping on the verge to take a photograph is not recommended. There is, however, a little parking area on the north side of the road where Bond lovers may stop and capture more or less the same spectacular view that we see on screen. The above postcode puts one in the correct general area, but for the precise location of the parking area, use National Grid

The A82 is the main road that takes visitors, including Bond, into the Highlands.

Reference NN286525 in consultation with Ordnance Survey mapping (for example Explorer maps 377 or 384). If not armed with the appropriate mapping, once you have passed the Loch Tulla viewpoint, continue towards Glencoe for about 7½km. You will then be entering the very straight piece of road, with the small parking area being on the right about 1½km further along. The area is not signposted, so go carefully and give yourself plenty of stopping distance. Take extra care of the very fast traffic when taking photographs.

Bridge of Orchy Hotel, Bridge of Orchy, Argyll and Bute, PA36 4AD
www.bridgeoforchy.co.uk

Even before he revealed Bond's Scottish heritage in *On Her Majesty's Secret Service*, expanding on it in *You Only Live Twice*, presumably having been encouraged by the coincidence of Scotsman Sean Connery being chosen to play his hero on screen, Ian Fleming had peppered his novels with references that reflected his own connections with Scotland. In *Thunderball*, for instance, Bond's housekeeper May, whom readers already knew from *Moonraker* as being Scottish, is identified as hailing from Glen Orchy. It is in Glen Orchy that Black Mount, an estate on the edge of Loch Tulla, is situated. As a child, Fleming would spend his late summers with the rest of the family at Black Mount, where deer stalking and game shooting were the usual pastimes. Aged 16, Ian shot his first stag, but he was never comfortable with the idea of hunting for sport and he excused himself from such activities when he could.

The hotel at Bridge of Orchy, a village on the A82, the main road from Glasgow

The Bridge of Orchy Hotel.

into the Highlands, makes a good base from which to explore 'Fleming country', and, indeed, it is not unreasonable to suppose that the Flemings dined at the hotel from time to time. The Bridge of Orchy itself is behind the hotel and offers splendid views of the glen. Black Mount is not open to the public, but the entrance to the drive leading to the house can be reached either on foot or vehicle. If going by foot, head north-west from the bridge for approximately 4½km along the Old Military Road and West Highland Way until you reach Forest Lodge just after Victoria Bridge (a copy of Ordnance Survey Explorer Map 377 is well recommended). If going by vehicle, turn right after the Bridge of Orchy, and follow the single-lane track north along the River Orchy and then

The drive leading to Black Mount, Bridge of Orchy.

round the west end of Loch Tulla until you reach a car park just before Victoria Bridge, then walk the remainder of the way to Forest Lodge. The entrance to the drive for Black Mount (nearest postcode: PA36 4AH), opposite Forest Lodge, will be on your right as you look north towards the continuation of the West Highland Way, also known as the old drove road to Glencoe. If, by this point, you are up for a little more hiking, head further along the West Highland Way to explore more of the Black Mount estate.

After returning to Bridge of Orchy, drive north along the A82 for about 7km to a viewpoint and parking area on a bend of the road (marked on the Ordnance Survey map) overlooking Loch Tulla for stunning views of the loch and the Flemings' former estate.

Lunga House, Craobh Haven, Argyll and Bute, PA31 8UU

www.lungahouse.co.uk

Lunga House, between the villages of Craobh Haven and Ardfern, took the place of a Balkan quayside when it was used for a scene in FROM RUSSIA WITH LOVE. Bond (Sean Connery) and Tatiana Romanova (Daniela Bianchi), having escaped a grenade-dropping SPECTRE helicopter, drive their commandeered florist's truck to a stone pier, then abandon the vehicle and hop into a boat, taking with them a hapless SPECTRE agent, whom Bond pushes into the water.

Lunga House is a coastal castle and estate that offers a wedding venue, holiday cottages, activities such as horse riding, and camping. The pier is located within the campsite, which is reached by driving past the stables, turning right and passing the estate office, and then turning right again to go down the hill to the water's edge. Before making their way to the campsite, which is well

The pier at Lunga House, made famous by FROM RUSSIA WITH LOVE.

signposted, I recommend that Bond lovers pop into the estate office to notify the staff of their wish to visit the pier. There should be no difficulty with access, and the staff are very welcoming, but the courtesy will be appreciated.

Ardfern Yacht Centre, Ardfern, Argyll and Bute, PA31 8QN

The west coast of Scotland doubled for the Balkans in several scenes of FROM RUSSIA WITH LOVE. Loch Craignish became the Adriatic Sea in the sequence where Bond (Sean Connery) and Tatiana Romanova (Daniela Bianchi), making their escape across the water towards Venice, are forced to evade SPECTRE agents. Bond manages to achieve this by dropping barrels of oil into the water and lighting them up with a flare gun. (Local residents were each paid a pound per day to help with the setting up of this sequence.) The

Loch Craignish was the scene of a boat chase in FROM RUSSIA WITH LOVE.

village of Ardfern is a good base from which to explore Loch Craignish. Park in the yacht centre for good views of the head of the loch.

Lechuary, Lochgilphead, Argyll and Bute, PA31 8LZ

FROM RUSSIA WITH LOVE is undoubtedly the most Hitchcockian of James Bond films, underlined by the scene set in the Balkan hills in which Bond (Sean Connery), pursued by a helicopter piloted by SPECTRE agents, runs for cover, falling to the ground as the helicopter swoops down. The scene paid tribute to Alfred Hitchcock's 1959 film, NORTH BY NORTHWEST, alluding specifically to the film's famous crop-duster scene that sees Roger O. Thornhill (Cary Grant) running from the path of a biplane and hitting the deck time after time as the plane dives down. Film producers Albert Broccoli and Harry Saltzman were not the only Bond creatives impressed by Hitchcock's film. Cultural historian Robert Sellers notes in his 2007 book, *The Battle for Bond*, that Ian Fleming saw the film on its release. He enjoyed it so much that he referenced the film in *Thunderball*; SPECTRE agent Giuseppe Petacchi, on board a

The hills of Lechuary saw a thrilling sequence that pitted Bond against SPECTRE agents in a helicopter.

Vindicator aircraft laden with atomic weapons and preparing to hijack the plane, regrets missing NORTH BY NORTHWEST at the Odeon.

The scene in FROM RUSSIA WITH LOVE was not filmed in the Balkans, but in the hills behind Lochgilphead on the west coast of Scotland. The location can be reached by coming off the A816 road on to a minor road toward Kilmartin Glassary. Continue through the village and along the minor, single-track road for about 3km until you arrive at the hamlet of Leckuary. Turn right on to a gravel track and continue east for just over a kilometre until you arrive at a fork in the road with a choice of two paths, both blocked by gates. (For those with Ordnance Survey maps, this is at National Grid Reference NR887956.) Park your vehicle here and proceed along the left-hand track up the hill by foot. Once you reach the top of the hill, after following the winding path, you will be standing in the landscape that was filmed for the helicopter scene.

HMNB Clyde, Faslane, Helensburgh, Argyll and Bute, G84 0EH

His Majesty's Naval Base Clyde on the edge of Gare Loch provided the backdrop for the sequence in THE SPY WHO LOVED ME when Bond (Roger Moore), appropriately attired in navy uniform – the stripes on the sleeve correctly identifying him as a commander – flies in for a briefing with M (Bernard Lee), Q (Desmond Llewelyn),

Roger Moore's James Bond comes to Gare Loch in THE SPY WHO LOVED ME.

the Minister of Defence Frederick Gray (Geoffrey Keen), Captain Benson (George Baker), and Admiral Hargreaves (Robert Brown), following the disappearance of the nuclear-armed submarine HMS *Ranger*. There, he learns that the plans of a submarine tracking system have been stolen. Bond and Gray discuss the situation further while walking along the quay of the naval base, providing the audience with views of the loch and a departing submarine.

The naval base is naturally closed to ordinary visitors, but viewpoints similar to those we see on screen, albeit obscured by fencing, may be gained from the A814 road that runs past the base, although stopping places are largely restricted to bus stops. For unrestricted views of the loch and better parking opportunities, then a visit to Garelochhead at the north end of the loch or Shandon, Rhu or Helensburgh south of the naval base is recommended.

Fettes College, Carrington Road, Edinburgh, EH4 1QX

In *You Only Live Twice*, M's obituary for Bond records that the young James, after some trouble with one of the school maids, was removed from Eton College and transferred to Fettes, his father's old school. There, he excelled in individual sports, particularly athletics, boxing and judo, just as Ian Fleming had done at Eton. Steve Cole, continuing the series of *Young Bond* novels begun by Charlie Higson, details some of the more

Fettes College. (Photo by Pawel Gieralt, CC BY-SA 4.0 https://creativecommons.org/licenses/by-sa/4.0, via Wikimedia Commons)

dramatic episodes of Bond's time at Fettes in *Strike Lightning*.

The school is not open to the public, but views of the main college block, a three-storey, mid-nineteenth-century, Franco–Scottish Gothic building, may be gained from the equally ornate school gates on Carrington Road.

Melvin Walk, Edinburgh, EH3 8EQ

It seems appropriate to conclude the *James Bond Lover's Guide to Britain* with a visit to the childhood home of the actor who introduced cinemagoers to Bond and helped make Ian Fleming's creation a worldwide cultural phenomenon. Sean Connery, born in 1930, was brought up at 176 Fountainbridge in Edinburgh. The tenement has long since been demolished, but a plaque commemorating his contribution to the film industry can be seen on Melvin Walk close to where he lived.

LIST OF JAMES BOND BOOKS AND FILMS

The James Bond Stories by Ian Fleming
Casino Royale (Jonathan Cape, London, 1953)

Live and Let Die (Jonathan Cape, London, 1954)

Moonraker (Jonathan Cape, London, 1955)

Diamonds Are Forever (Jonathan Cape, London, 1956)

From Russia With Love (Jonathan Cape, London, 1957)

Dr No (Jonathan Cape, London, 1958)

Goldfinger (Jonathan Cape, London, 1959)

For Your Eyes Only (Jonathan Cape, London, 1960)

Thunderball (Jonathan Cape, London, 1961)

The Spy Who Loved Me (Jonathan Cape, London, 1962)

On Her Majesty's Secret Service (Jonathan Cape, London, 1963)

You Only Live Twice (Jonathan Cape, London, 1964)

The Man with the Golden Gun (Jonathan Cape, London, 1965)

Octopussy and The Living Daylights (Jonathan Cape, London, 1966)

The current editions of all titles were published in 2023 by Ian Fleming Publications.

The EON-produced James Bond films
Dr No (directed by Terence Young, written by Richard Maibaum, Johanna Harwood and Berkely Mather, produced by Albert R. Broccoli and Harry Saltzman, 1962)

From Russia With Love (directed by Terence Young, written by Richard Maibaum and Johanna Harwood, produced by Albert R. Broccoli and Harry Saltzman, 1963)

Goldfinger (directed by Guy Hamilton, written by Richard Maibaum and Paul Dehn, produced by Albert R. Broccoli and Harry Saltzman, 1964)

Thunderball (directed by Terence Young, written by Richard Maibaum and John Hopkins, based on an original screen story by Jack Whittingham and an original story by Jack Whittingham, Kevin McClory and Ian Fleming, produced by Kevin McClory, 1965)

You Only Live Twice (directed by Lewis Gilbert, written by Harold Jack Bloom and Roald Dahl, produced by Albert R. Broccoli and Harry Saltzman, 1967)

On Her Majesty's Secret Service (directed by Peter R. Hunt, written by Richard Maibaum, produced by Albert R. Broccoli and Harry Saltzman, 1969)

Diamonds Are Forever (directed by Guy Hamilton, written by Richard Maibaum and Tom Mankiewicz, produced by Albert R. Broccoli and Harry Saltzman, 1971)

Live and Let Die (directed by Guy Hamilton, written by Tom Mankiewicz, produced by Albert R. Broccoli and Harry Saltzman, 1973)

The Man with the Golden Gun (directed by Guy Hamilton, written by Richard Maibaum and Tom Mankiewicz, produced by Albert R. Broccoli and Harry Saltzman, 1974)

The Spy Who Loved Me (directed by Lewis Gilbert, written by Christopher Wood and Richard Maibaum, produced by Albert R. Broccoli, 1977)

Moonraker (directed by Lewis Gilbert, written by Christopher Wood, produced by Albert R. Broccoli, 1979)

For Your Eyes Only (directed by John Glen, written by Richard Maibaum and Michael G. Wilson, produced by Albert R. Broccoli, 1981)

Octopussy (directed by John Glen, written by George MacDonald Fraser, Richard Maibaum and Michael G. Wilson, produced by Albert R. Broccoli, 1983)

A View To A Kill (directed by John Glen, written by Richard Maibaum and Michael G. Wilson, produced by Albert R. Broccoli, 1985)

The Living Daylights (directed by John Glen, written by Richard Maibaum and Michael G. Wilson, produced by Albert R. Broccoli, 1987)

Licence to Kill (directed by John Glen, written by Michael G. Wilson and Richard Maibaum, produced by Albert R. Broccoli, 1989)

GoldenEye (directed by Martin Campbell, written by Michael France, Jeffrey Caine and Bruce Feirstein, produced by Albert R. Broccoli, Barbara Broccoli and Michael G. Wilson, 1995)

Tomorrow Never Dies (directed by Roger Spottiswoode, written by Bruce Feirstein, produced by Barbara Broccoli and Michael G. Wilson, 1997)

The World is Not Enough (directed by Michael Apted, written by Bruce Feirstein, Neal Purvis and Robert Wade, produced by Barbara Broccoli and Michael G. Wilson, 1999)

Die Another Day (directed by Lee Tamahori, written by Neal Purvis and Robert Wade, produced by Barbara Broccoli and Michael G. Wilson, 2002)

Casino Royale (directed by Martin Campbell, written by Neal Purvis and Robert Wade, and Paul Haggis, produced by Barbara Broccoli and Michael G. Wilson, 2006)

Quantum of Solace (directed by Marc Forster, written by Paul Haggis, Neal Purvis and Robert Wade, produced by Barbara Broccoli and Michael G. Wilson, 2008)

Skyfall (directed by Sam Mendes, written by Neal Purvis and Robert Wade, and John Logan, produced by Barbara Broccoli and Michael G. Wilson, 2012)

Spectre (directed by Sam Mendes, written by John Logan, Neal Purvis and Robert Wade, and Jez Butterworth, produced by Barbara Broccoli and Michael G. Wilson, 2015)

No Time To Die (directed by Cary Joji Fukunaga, written by Neal Purvis and Robert Wade, Cary Joji Fukunaga, and Phoebe Waller-Bridge, produced by Barbara Broccoli and Michael G. Wilson, 2021)

Other James Bond films

Casino Royale (directed by John Huston, Ken Hughes, Val Guest, Robert Parrish, and Joe McGrath, screenplay by Wolf Mankowitz, John Law and Michael Sayers, produced by Charles K. Feldman and John Bresler, 1967)

Never Say Never Again (directed by Irvin Kershner, screenplay by Lorenzo Semple Jr based on an original story by Kevin McClory, Jack Whittingham and Ian Fleming, produced by Jack Schwartzman, with executive producer Kevin McClory, 1983)

BIBLIOGRAPHY AND FURTHER READING

Amory, M. (ed.), *The Letters of Ann Fleming* (Collins Harvill, London, 1985)

Anon., *St Margaret's Village History*, www.stmargaretshistory.org.uk

Barlow, J., *Bond Cars: The Definitive History* (Penguin, London, 2020)

Bucknall, R., *Boat Trains and Channel Packets: The English Short Sea Routes* (Vincent Stuart Ltd, London, 1957)

Cole, S., *Strike Lightning* (Doubleday, London, 2016)

Edlitz, M., *The Many Lives of James Bond* (Lyons Press, Lanham, MD, 2019)

Field, M., and Chowdhury, A., *Some Kind of Hero: The Remarkable Story of the James Bond Films* (The History Press, Stroud, 2015)

Fleming, I., *Talk of the Devil* (Queen Anne Press, London, 2008)

Fleming, I., *Chitty Chitty Bang Bang* (Ian Fleming Publications, London, 2024)

Harling, R., *Ian Fleming: A Personal Memoir* (The Robson Press, London, 2015)

Hernu, S., *Q: The Biography of Desmond Llewelyn* (S.B. Publications, Seaford, 1999)

Higson, C., *SilverFin* (Puffin, London, 2005)

Historic England, *The National Heritage List for England* (https://historicengland.org.uklisting/the-list)

IMDb, *Internet Movie Database* (imdb.com)

Jones, T., *Over the Top and Back* (Penguin, London, 2016)

Lycett, A., *Ian Fleming: The Man Behind James Bond* (Turner, Atlanta, 1995)

Moore, R., with Owen, G., *My Word is My Bond: The Autobiography* (Michael O'Mara Books, London, 2008)

Mulder, M., and Kloosterboer, D., *On the Tracks of 007: A Field Guide to the Exotic James Bond Filming Locations Around the World* (DMD Digital, 2008)

Pearson, J., *The Life of Ian Fleming, Creator of James Bond* (Jonathan Cape, London, 1966)

Pearson, J., *James Bond: The Authorized Biography of James Bond* (Sidgwick & Jackson, London, 1973)

Sellers, R., *The Battle for Bond: The Genesis of Cinema's Greatest Hero* (Tomahawk Press, Sheffield, 2007)

Shakespeare, N., *Ian Fleming: The Complete Man* (Harvill Secker, London, 2023)

Sherwood, K., *A Spy Like Me* (Hemlock Press, London, 2024)

Sherwood, J., and Pevsner, N., *Oxfordshire* (New Haven, London, 2002)

Snowman, A.K., *The Art of Carl Fabergé* (Faber & Faber, London, 1953)

Turner, J.L., *The Visitors' Book. In Francis Bacon's Shadow: The Lives of Richard Chopping and Denis Wirth-Miller* (Constable, London, 2016)